Other Books by Gostick and Elton:

The Invisible Employee
A Carrot a Day
The 24-Carrot Manager

Books by Gostick and Dana Telford

The Integrity Advantage
Integrity Works

THE CARROT PRINCIPLE

*How the best managers use recognition
to engage their people, retain talent,
and accelerate performance*

Adrian Gostick
and Chester Elton

FREE PRESS
New York London Toronto Sydney

FREE PRESS
A Division of Simon & Schuster, Inc.
1230 Avenue of the Americas
New York, NY 10020

First Free Press Export Edition 2007

FREE PRESS and colophon are trademarks
of Simon & Schuster, Inc.

For information about special discounts for bulk purchases,
please contact Simon & Schuster Special Sales: 1-800-456-6798
or business@simonandschuster.com.

Designed by Jaime Putorti

Manufactured in the United States of America

10 9 8 7 6 5 4 3 2 1

ISBN-13: 978-1-4165-4417-3
ISBN-10:   1-4165-4417-8

To our families for their long-suffering natures, tireless support, and, most important, their love.

To Jennifer and Tony.

To Heidi, Cassi, Carter, Brinden, and Garrett.

You are our heroes.

CONTENTS

PART I: THE ACCELERATOR

How the Best Managers Deliver Extraordinary Results

PART II: CARROT CULTURE

How Great Organizations Create World-Class Results

PART III: MANAGING BY CARROTS

You Can Get There from Here

THE ACCELERATOR

*How the Best Managers
Deliver Extraordinary Results*

1

A Missing Ingredient

Striding home from the local mercantile, Charles Goodyear glanced down at a charred piece of India rubber in his hands and hoped it wouldn't be another dead end. It was 1839. For five roller-coaster years, he had searched for the missing ingredient that would stabilize rubber. Had he finally found it? It was a little frightening, really, to be teetering on the edge of something revolutionary like this, especially considering how many times he had come this far and failed.

Goodyear's first brush with fortune had come when he was just twenty-six. He had set up the first hardware store in America to sell domestically manufactured farm implements. The timing was right, and the venture was successful. In fact, it was doubly successful from Goodyear's perspective: not only did he own the store, he was a partner in the firm that produced many of the implements sold there.

Everyone, including Goodyear, agreed that fortune and fame were his for the taking—everyone, that is, except fate. Within three years, several of Goodyear's American suppliers closed their doors. Goodyear, who had been just inches from wild success, served the first of many sentences in debtors' prison.

About the same time, rubber companies around the country were universally closing their doors. Although the new waterproof gum elastic from Brazil had captivated the public when introduced, it was untested and had a lot of bugs. In the heat, rubber products became soft, sticky, and smelly. In the cold, they became hard and brittle and often cracked.

But while most were giving up on rubber, Goodyear became fascinated by the substance and the challenge of stabilizing it. The waterproof gum from Brazil was cheap enough for him to purchase even while in debtors' prison. With little to occupy his time, he spent hours working it with his wife's rolling pin, though with no success. Once out of prison, he tried mixing the rubber with magnesia and lampblack dissolved in turpentine. Next, he combined the rubber with magnesia and boiled it in quicklime and water. Over the next five years, Goodyear tried hundreds of experiments. Then one day, he rubbed nitric acid on a sample of rubber to remove its coating of bronze paint. It turned the sample black, but also made it smooth and dry and almost clothlike. The acid, it turned out, was a curing agent.

It seemed to work so well, in fact, that the U.S. Post Office in Boston ordered 150 rubber mailbags cured with nitric acid in the hope that waterproof bags would protect the mail from rain and snow during delivery. Goodyear made the mailbags, then stored them while he took his family on a celebratory vacation. They returned to find the bags had rotted in the warm storage room; the acid had cured only the rubber's surface, leaving the interior to decompose.

The year 1839 was difficult. The Goodyear children dug in the neighboring farmer's fields for potatoes to eat. Farmers gave them free milk. Many times that winter Goodyear considered giving up, but then he would experience a minor breakthrough, and success would seem so close that he had to continue.

And now, after five long years, it seemed he had done it. He stopped in the winter night to examine the charred piece of rubber in his hand. How had it happened? The last few moments were a blur.

He had gone to the mercantile to demonstrate his new mixture of rubber and sulfur to the men gathered there. When they laughed at him, he responded in disgust, forcefully flipping a small piece of the rubber-sulfur mixture in his hand onto the nearby stove. He wanted to storm from the store, but rubber and sulfur cost money. So he went to the stove to pick up the piece he imagined had melted on the hot surface. But instead of softening, the rubber had charred like leather, and on the edge of the charred section was a brown rim, where the rubber had perfectly cured.

Heat was what had been missing.

The transformation of rubber from a useless substance to a resilient product was as simple as adding a missing process— heat, in the form of steam. Goodyear named the process *vulcanization* after the Roman god of fire, Vulcan.

Today it's hard to imagine life without Goodyear's rubber. There would be no electricity, no cars, no computers, no bicycles, no radios or televisions, no phones. We wouldn't have airplanes, washing machines, or toasters. We wouldn't even have our favorite pair of old sneakers.

Years later, those chronicling his life called Goodyear's moment of discovery an accident. Goodyear strongly disagreed. He argued that if he had not "applied himself most perseveringly to the subject," the accident would have had no meaning. He asserted that he was the only man "whose mind was prepared to draw an inference" from the incident. In other words, he was prepared and ready to go when the rubber hit the sizzling, pot-bellied stove.

Goodyear was a visionary. Not only could he see a future that others could not, he was the only man in a crowded room to recognize the introduction of heat to sulfur and rubber for what it was—a revolutionary, transformational *acceleration* process.

We've found that in business, there are leaders who are visionaries. They see the untapped potential of their workforces and believe it is possible to reach higher. They have spent years experimenting with their leadership styles. They have consulted mentors, read business books, and attended seminars. Through their efforts, they have brought their employees a long way toward reaching their maximum potential—but not all the way. And there's the rub.

Show us any leader who sets clear goals, communicates openly, respects people and treats them fairly, holds people accountable, and creates trusting relationships, and we'll show you a leader who's *almost* got it right.

Show us an organization where people are coming to work on time, doing their jobs, and feel satisfied, and we'll show you an organization that is *close* to achieving its full potential.

Show us some good management books that promise to transform your organization from ordinary to extraordinary, and we'll show you wisdom that will push you *nearer* to your goals than you've ever gotten before.

Almost. Closer. Nearer. Some would argue that they are good words. For some leaders, they might even be good enough. But for those of us who are determined to reach beyond the ordinary to our maximum potential, "almost there" is a frustrating place to be.

What we need is an accelerator.

Scientists have known the secret of accelerants for decades, adding them to speed up chemical reactions, achieving results more quickly. Accelerators work the same way in business, making the things you're doing work better, faster, and more smoothly, without throwing you (or your organization) off balance.

It may sound like magic, but it isn't. The relationship between a management accelerant and improved business results is highly predictable. In fact, an accelerant is the missing ingredient that will bridge the gap between where your team is now and where it can be. And in the workplace, there is no accelerator with more impact than purpose-based recognition. The numbers prove it.

First, the Research

Our guts always told us that acceleration was the answer. During the past fifteen years, we have visited more than two dozen countries, taught seminars to almost a million people, and spent thousands of hours consulting with leaders of Fortune 500 titans. Through that time, we have repeatedly witnessed the power of recognition to improve not only morale but business results as well. But what we really needed—and what drives businesses in general—is unmistakable empirical evidence. That evidence is what makes this book unique. Here are just a few preview insights from our research that might startle you:

- In response to the question "My organization recognizes excellence," the organizations that scored in the lowest fourth overall had an average return on equity (ROE) of 2.4 percent, whereas those that scored in the top fourth had an average ROE of 8.7 percent. In other words, companies that most effectively recognize excellence enjoy a return that is more than triple the return of those that do so the worst.

- The teams and offices rated most highly by employees in response to, "My manager does a good job of recognizing employee contributions," also typically place in the top scores for customer satisfaction, employee satisfaction, and retention.

- Of the people who report the highest morale at work, 94.4 percent agree that their managers are effective at recognition. In contrast, 56 percent of employees who report low morale give their manager a failing grade on recognition, and only 2.4 percent of people who have low morale say they have a boss who is great at recognition.

Numbers like these are the result of one of the most extensive and in-depth studies ever conducted on workplace productivity, involving ten years of research by The Jackson Organization and 200,000 interviews with managers and their employees around the globe. Employing a large team of expert researchers, analysts, and consultants, The Jackson Organization collaborated with us to quantify the connections among employee satisfaction, business outcomes, and recognition.

Our primary research tool was surveys, but pure numbers can be cold and uninspiring, so in addition, to cull the emotions and thoughts behind the data, we conducted several dozen focus groups in five major metropolitan cities where we met with groups of line managers from all industries. And finally, throughout 2005 and well into 2006, we conducted one-on-one interviews with hundreds of managers and their employees, primarily in the United States and Canada, but also in the United Kingdom, Germany, China, South Africa, Singapore, Malaysia, Thailand, and Turkey. (For more detail about the studies, see the appendices.)

And after all this research? What we have found about motivation, effective management, and the impact of the accelerator is actually quite remarkable. We think Goodyear would be proud.

So if you're tired of *almost* achieving your potential, if coming *close* isn't *nearly* good enough anymore, let's shift things into high gear. Get ready to accelerate.

Not-So-Soft Recognition

Lying idle. That's exactly what the recognition accelerator has been doing in many organizations for much too long. Like heat in Goodyear's innovation, it's been here for a long time: overlooked, misapplied, misunderstood, and largely untapped. The fact is that 79 percent of employees who quit their jobs cite a lack of appreciation as a key reason for leaving. Sixty-five percent of North Americans report that they weren't recognized in the least bit the previous year.

The simple but transformative act of a leader expressing appreciation to a person in a meaningful and memorable way is the missing accelerator that can do so much and yet is used so sparingly. But it is not the employee recognition some of us have been using for years. Not by a long shot. This is purpose-based recognition. It is recognition done right, recognition within a context of effective leadership. And as the most dramatic accelerator of human potential, it's the most effective carrot.

What is a carrot? For a successful leader, it's an acceleration tool. Our *Oxford English Dictionary* calls it "something enticing offered as a means of persuasion." In business, a carrot is something used to inspire and motivate an employee. It's something to be desired. In fact, it tops the list of things employees say they want most from their employers. Simply put, when employees know that their strengths and potential will be praised and recognized, they are significantly more likely to produce value.

Yet some will ask, "Isn't money the most effective carrot? Aren't the allure of bonuses and increases in salary what really motivate our employees?"

The fact is that money is not as powerful a reward as many people think. While pay and bonuses must be competitive to attract and retain talented employees, smaller amounts of cash— anything short of $1,000—will never make the best rewards because they are so easily forgotten.

In fact one-third of the people you give a cash award to will use that money to pay bills. Another one in five won't have any clue in a few months where they spent the money or even how much they received. Just ask yourself, did you save the bank deposit slip from the last time someone gave you a $200 cash bonus? Is it tucked away in a scrapbook of memories? Of course not. But what about something useful and tangible that was given to you as a reward? Not a baseball cap, T-shirt, or canvas tote bag, but something usable and valuable. Chances are that even years later, you still own it and can picture the award in your mind.

The more prevalent problem with cash is that the supply is

limited and strictly controlled, and your people know it. For many of the managers reading this book, that might not be the case. Many of us in middle and senior leadership roles are indeed motivated by the allure of a large bonus or increase in salary. Hefty sums of cash may in fact be motivating to us. But realize that for the majority of the people in your charge, that's just not in their cards. And here's why: no matter what they do, your employees know you have only so much cash to share with them. Pay, for example, is determined by the employee's experience, job type, higher corporate policy, location, and other factors outside your and your employees' control. If an employee is doing a fantastic job, you might be able to swing a 5 percent raise at the end of the year. Not much motivation there. As for large bonuses tied to personal performance, they are typically reserved for mid- to upper-level leaders. Lower-level employees and professional staff typically receive a standard bonus amount, with very little variation from person to person. Not a lot of motivation to excel there either. Benefits too are locked in. As a manager, you can hardly offer an excellent employee a better dental plan.

The happy surprises of pay and benefits that a motivated employee hopes for are frequently beyond your control to provide. The reality is that most workers are locked into a routine of sameness, paycheck to paycheck. So it's time to learn what you do control: the carrot supply.

"When people join us, they obviously have agreed on the pay," said Elizabeth Martin-Chua, vice president of Philips Electronics in Singapore. "What they are hoping for is a good environment where they can use their capabilities and talent to good advantage and then be recognized for it."

Martin-Chua's comments are backed up by a study by HRM Singapore, which in December 2005 interviewed 3,000 people in this highly developed country on the South China Sea. When asked, "What do you really want from your job?" employees ranked "Pay" number three on their list. Number one was "Career/Learning Development Opportunities." Number two?

"Recognition." Interestingly, number four was a better "Relationship with Manager." According to the editors, "The economic success of Singapore means that employees need more than pay to be motivated."

And that leads us to the key finding of the 200,000-person study by The Jackson Organization: the central characteristic of truly effective management—the element that shows up time and again in every great workplace—is a manager's ability to recognize employees' talents and contributions in a *purposeful* manner. Our study results show that when recognition is considered effective, managers:

1. Have lower turnover rates

2. Achieve enhanced business results

3. Are seen as much stronger in what we call the Basic Four areas of leadership:

   - Goal setting

   - Communication

   - Trust

   - Accountability

In other words, recognition accelerates a leader's effectiveness. Dee Hansford, former head of Walt Disney World's cast recognition department, can attest to the difference purpose-based recognition can make. In 1996, the theme park was very busy. With a twenty-fifth anniversary celebration, the park experienced a 15 percent rise in guest attendance. Despite the increased traffic, that year no pay raises or bonuses were given. Under such conditions, you might think employee satisfaction would have fallen off the charts. Instead, employee job satisfaction rose 15 percent.

The difference was the recognition skills training Hansford and her team had given to more than 6,000 managers and super-

visors. Now, frontline leaders had the ability to praise operator
Steve for keeping people happy when a ride went down for maintenance, recognize the restaurant staff for making the kitchen
sparkle, or thank Goofy for being especially . . . well . . . goofy
that day.

Disney might have considered the year a success simply on
the basis of employee morale alone. But there was even more
magic in store: at the end of the year, Disney's annual report
showed a 15 percent increase in revenues directly attributable to
the theme park—in a year without a bonus or a raise given.

Watching the impact of recognition on a company is a bit
like watching the center pole lift up the middle of a large tent:
everything else rises too except one thing—turnover. With effective recognition, that can drop like a rock.

Retention *Accelerated*

Like a black hole in space, corporate turnover absorbs resources
at an astonishing rate. It is far and away the most significant un-
calculated expense in corporate America. Some estimates to re-
place a departing employee range up to a stunning 250 percent
of that person's annual salary. In this case, a little prevention is
definitely worth a pound of cure. According to author Fred
Reichheld, just a 5 percent increase in employee loyalty can increase profits by as much as 50 percent.

The reason turnover has such a high cost has to do with the
type of people who are leaving. If most of the people who left
were poor performers, turnover would be a good thing. But it's
not. Organizations that fail to effectively recognize their employees are losing the very workers they wish they could keep to
meet their goals.

Turnover is an estimated $5 trillion annual drain on the U.S.
economy, making it the most significant cost to its economy and
one of the most ignored economic factors in business history.
Compounding the problem is the fact that with the global economy heating up, the shortage of skilled, talented workers is

growing even more severe. By 2008, the U.S. Bureau of Labor Statistics predicts a shortfall of 10 million workers in America. That means we are all in a race for talent, and the best place to find talent is under our noses. We must retain our solid and our outstanding performers by keeping them engaged. And yet some 75 percent of the U.S. workforce is not fully engaged on the job. The United States is not alone in this predicament. In the United Kingdom, surveys show that more than 80 percent of workers lack real commitment to their jobs. Estimates of the cost of disengaged workers on the British economy range between 37 and 39 billion pounds sterling per year.

An insidious result of turnover is the psychological damage to the employees who stay. Turnover decimates the remaining workplace because many employees mentally follow their departing colleagues: they worry about their futures, passively wait for things to get better, or actively look for new positions.

It is becoming increasingly difficult for leaders to ignore the destructive impact of turnover. In our travels, a majority of the CEOs and senior leaders we work with cite retention of key employees as the most important factor to their success—not one of but *the* key factor.

In response to the slow bleed, many leaders and organizations have sought to remedy matters. The Society for Human Resource Management periodically surveys employers on retention initiatives. Common initiatives include tuition reimbursement, competitive vacation and holiday benefits, higher pay, and better employee selection methods. The results of such perks and methods on employee trust levels have been underwhelming at best, to the consternation of the leaders who designed them. "Why isn't it working?" managers wonder. "After all, we're giving employees what they want." And there's the problem: employers don't know what employees really want.

A fascinating survey has been conducted three times since 1949, when author Lawrence Lindahl first began studying human behavior at work. Each time the results have been the same. In the survey, managers were asked to name what they thought employees in their organizations wanted. Then management's list was contrasted with the list prepared by employees. Every time, managers guessed that good wages and job security would top employee lists, but their people always cited "feeling appreciated" and "informed." While a serious disconnect exists, it's clear what employees really want.

So what *is* working? Overwhelming research points the finger at recognition. A Watson Wyatt Reward Plan Survey of 614 employers with 3.5 million employees showed that the average turnover rate of employers with a clear reward strategy is 13 percent lower than that of organizations without one. In addition, Gallup's study of nearly 5 million employees reveals that an increase in recognition and praise in an organization can lead to lower turnover, higher customer loyalty and satisfaction scores, and increases in overall productivity. And U.S. Department of Labor statistics show the number one reason people leave organizations is that they "don't feel appreciated."

Perks like tuition reimbursement can never take the place of a frontline supervisor who sets clear goals, communicates, builds trust, holds employees accountable, and then recognizes in an effective manner.

That's what KPMG LLP, the U.S. audit, tax, and advisory firm, discovered when it implemented its national recognition program, Encore. By providing managers with a formal way to recognize their employees and teams, the firm has improved overall employee survey scores.

On its annual work environment survey, KPMG asks, "Taking everything into account, this a great place to work." In the three years since the introduction of an effective recognition system, positive employee scores on that question have increased more than 20 points. Now, it's important to note that the three years in question were also a time of tremendous scrutiny and pressure for the accounting industry, with employee satisfaction in most of these firms nearing all-time lows.

Sylvia Brandes, director of compensation for KPMG's 19,000 U.S. employees says, "Recognition has become a fever."

She adds that KPMG has done its homework through analysis of the effectiveness of its recognition efforts. "What we found is that groups that do not present a lot of Encores [awards] in their organizations tend to have greater turnover. We also found turnover among people who received an award was half that of those who hadn't received an award. And we found a correlation between functions or organizations that had higher scores for recognition and the number of Encore awards that were given within that group."

Business Results *Accelerated*

KPMG's results are far from unique. Research firm Watson Wyatt has asked employees to identify "very significant" motivators of performance, and 66 percent said "appreciation." The numbers come as no surprise, as many of us might naturally expect an accelerator like recognition to affect motivation.

Then our researchers at The Jackson Organization made an important discovery within their data of a highly pecuniary nature. While the research consultants had always seen recognition as a key driver of employee engagement and satisfaction, they had never cut the data to test for a connection between effective recognition and business outcomes. When they did, the result was startling: from every angle, every financial metric, every way of looking at it, investing in recognizing excellence is strongly associated with the best financial performance.

The major study included 26,000 employees at all levels in thirty-one organizations of varying sizes and profitability. As part of the study, these organizations allowed researchers to conduct not only an in-depth employee survey, but also to dig into their financial reports. Some companies were very profitable; others were not. Some had engaged workforces; others did not. The sample size and variance of company profitability and engagement created data that are statistically unquestionable.

In addition to answering general questions about their level of engagement with their firms, employee respondents stated their level of agreement on a scale to the question: "My organization recognizes excellence." The responses by organization were averaged and grouped into four quarters. Those organizational results were then compared with these profitability measures: return on equity, return on assets, and operating margin.

Recognition and Return on Equity

Return on equity (ROE) is a critical measure that encompasses profitability, asset management, and financial leverage. Calculated by taking the fiscal year's earnings and dividing them by the average shareholder's equity for that year, it is used as a general indication of how much profit a company is able to generate given the investment provided by its shareholders.

According to the data, companies that effectively recognize excellence enjoy an ROE more than three times higher than the return experienced by firms that do not. But that's not all, not by a long shot.

ROE PERFORMANCE BY QUARTILE ON
"MY ORGANIZATION RECOGNIZES EXCELLENCE"

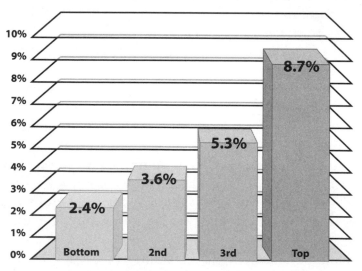

Recognition and Return on Assets

An equivalent connection is shown between recognition and return on assets (ROA), a fiscal year's earnings divided by total assets. This is a good measure of a firm's effectiveness in using the assets at hand to generate earnings. According to the data, companies that effectively recognize excellence enjoy an ROA more than three times higher than the return experienced by firms that don't.

ROE PERFORMANCE BY QUARTILE ON "MY ORGANIZATION RECOGNIZES EXCELLENCE"

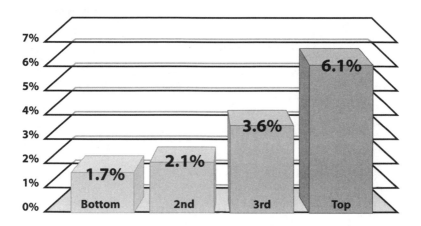

Recognition and Operating Margin

Operating margin is another measurement of an organization's profitability and efficiency. The ratio of operating income to sales, operating margin shows how much a company makes from each dollar of sales before interest and taxes. In general, businesses with higher operating margins tend to have lower costs and better gross margins. That gives them more pricing flexibility and an added measure of safety during tough economic times.

Of all the financial measurements, employee recognition has

the most significant impact on operating margin. According to the data, companies in the highest quartile of recognition of excellence report an operating margin of 6.6 percent, while those in the lowest quartile report 1 percent.

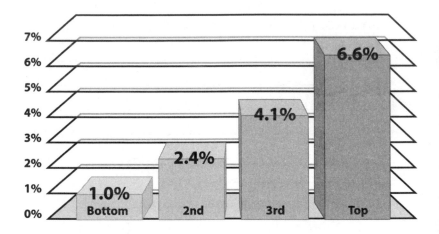

OPERATING MARGIN PERFORMANCE BY QUARTILE ON "MY ORGANIZATION RECOGNIZES EXCELLENCE"

Of this research, Karen Endresen, Ph.D. of The Jackson Organization, said, "Up until this study, the link between recognition and financial performance was largely anecdotal. Recognition was considered by some to be an emotional afterthought, while those who believed that effective recognition would drive results had no hard data to prove it. This study took recognition results from myth to reality—from the soft side of business to a proven business essential."

It is a simple truth: we work harder at places where we feel recognized and valued for our unique contributions. And valued and engaged employees bring great value and profit to their organizations.

What these data show us, in a very dramatic way, is that recognition is one of the key characteristics of effective managers and great organizations. But before we can understand how it accelerates performance, we must grasp the other characteristics of great management: the Basic Four.

2

The Basic Four of Leadership

On June 6, 1954, Englishman Roger Bannister did something most people at the time thought was physically impossible: he ran a mile in less than 4 minutes (to be more precise, in 3 minutes 59.4 seconds). The whole world erupted into celebration of the "miracle mile." There were newspaper and television articles. Bannister's face was on magazine covers and cereal boxes. There were even rumors that he would be knighted by the queen (he was in 1975). And every celebration of Bannister's record guaranteed that it would not be long before someone else would break it.

It happened one month later. The achievement that had taken all of human history to attain was suddenly left in the dust when Bannister's rival, John Landy of Australia, ran a mile in 3 minutes 58 seconds. The floodgate was open, and soon a sub-four mile became less a miracle than an expectation of top runners. What had accelerated the pace? Recognition. Bannister's achievement had shown the rest of the pack what was possible—with the attendant rewards and acclaim.

Recognition has a similarly accelerating impact in the workplace. It gives coworkers a vision of the possible and the desire to garner the rewards. But recognition isn't the only answer. Before there can be recognition, the basics have to be in place. In Bannister's case, he had to have innate talent, had to dedicate himself to a training regime, and had to run hundreds (maybe thousands) of races.

Some leaders in their enthusiasm for recognition miss this point. In sharing the results of our research, we've had leaders ask us, "So if a manager who is not trusted begins using recognition, will his trust scores go up?" Unfortunately that's a stretch. Recognition certainly helps. But if you haven't mastered the basics of leadership, you most likely don't have the foundational basis for employees to accept and react well to recognition. After all, would you accept praise from someone you didn't trust or from a manager who hardly ever communicates with you? No more than you could pull on your sweats right now and run a four-minute mile.

And that leads us again to the 200,000-person study by The Jackson Organization, which confirms that managers who achieve enhanced business results are significantly more likely to be seen by their employees as strong in what we call the Basic Four areas of leadership:

- Goal setting

- Communication

- Trust

- Accountability

The good news is that when a manager is even somewhat competent with the Basic Four and then adds the accelerator to each, management effectiveness soars in each characteristic.

Consider the question, "My manager recognizes excellence," in The Jackson Organization study (see the table on the next page). When respondents rated managers highly in this regard, the marks for leadership's Basic Four (goal setting, open communication, building trust, and accountability) are also rated extremely high. Remember that any correlation above a .50 is considered strong. (For those of us removed from college statistics, Pearson's correlation coefficients fall from positive at +1, to neutral at 0, and to negative at -1.) Let's use the first correlation under "trust" as an example. An employee who says her manager is effective at praise and recognition is almost guaranteed to say, "I trust my manager," since the correlation is an astoundingly high +0.76 (a correlation of 0.76 is more than simply strong, considering that a correlation of .30 is considered significant by statisticians). Now take a quick glance over these data and see how employees rate their managers in other areas when they are effective at recognition:

Goal Setting

- My manager gives me measurable   .70
  goals to achieve.

Communication

- I can rely on my manager to answer   .74
  my questions.

- My manager listens to employees   .74
  in our department.

- My manager keeps me informed   .70
  of the progress of my performance.

- My manager shares all the information   .70
  my coworkers and I need to feel part of the team.

- My manager is available when   .69
  workers need to talk.

- My manager encourages me to suggest   .69
  new ideas and methods for doing things.

- I feel completely free to express my views   .69
  to my manager.

- My coworkers' ideas are often accepted   .66
  by my manager.

- My opinions matter to my manager.   .75

- My manager encourages and supports   .67
  my learning and growth.

Trust

- I trust my immediate manager.   .76

- I trust my department's head.   .66

- My manager is fair to all employees.   .76

- My manager treats employees as more   .76
  than "just a number" or a
  "cog in the wheel."

- My manager treats me with respect.   .73

- I believe my manager cares about   .72
  me as a person.

- My manager stresses the importance   .70
  of teamwork.

Accountability

- My manager holds everyone in our   .64
  department accountable for their work.

In the entire list, the lowest score was +0.64, which cements the fact that the Basic Four and recognition have a stronger correlation than any other business grouping.

For a manager, the bottom line is this: *great management is born when recognition is added to the other characteristics of leadership*. This is the Carrot Principle. It is a simple concept, but one that works every time.

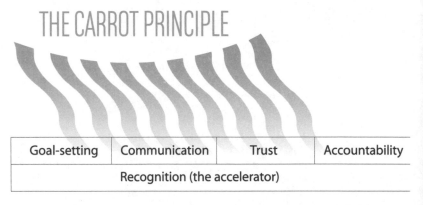

Goal-setting	Communication	Trust	Accountability
Recognition (the accelerator)			

In other words, when recognition is applied to the Basic Four of good management (goal setting, communication, trust, and accountability), it serves as an accelerator of employee performance and engagement.

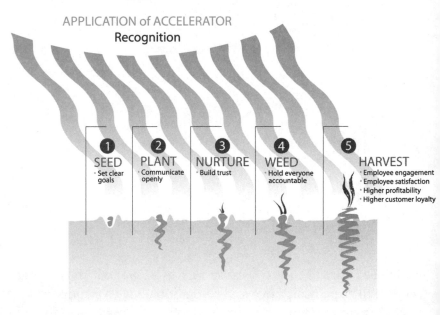

We see it as a process of growing a person and an organization toward vital goals.

The Basic Four Examined

There's a little bit of Charles Goodyear in every effective leader. If you can't see it, just think of all the seminars you've attended. Add up all the skills you have acquired. Count the business books you've read. See what we mean? All these good things you are already doing are like the mixtures that Goodyear stirred up on the stove. Over the years, you have created your own mix of leadership skills. The question is, Is it the right mix?

Our data culled from a decade of research show that goal setting, communication, trust, and accountability are the foundational building blocks of effective management. The numbers illustrate clearly that without these Basic Four elements, managers are dramatically less effective.

Now, some solid managers are good at one or two elements of the four. Perhaps they decide to earn their employees' trust by being a confidant. Or perhaps they focus on enhancing relationships by being a great communicator. Or they pride themselves on being the taskmaster who holds everyone accountable. We actually heard one manager say in a focus group, "I'm Joe Accountability."

Other managers are quite effective on all the Basic Four: they set goals, communicate frequently, build trusting relationships, and hold people accountable. But because they never say thanks in an effective way, they don't close the loop.

What all these well-intentioned people miss is that great managers do *all* of the Basic Four well, and they keep everything moving forward with a subtle undercurrent of recognition.

Throughout conducting our research, when we have found leaders strategically using praise and recognition in concert with all of leadership's Basic Four, employees are dramatically more engaged in their work and more satisfied with their jobs and with their leaders and their companies. The result is that team and company profitability is substantially higher.

Lee Elliot, vice president of human resources and development for St. Francis Hospital in Grand Island, Nebraska, is one of those great managers who realizes the impact of the Basic Four and recognition on his organization. This hospital has won national and international awards for recruitment innovation and employee retention while competing against Fortune 500 corporations with a lot more funding and resources. In the most recent employee satisfaction survey, Lee's division placed number 1 in satisfaction and nearly the highest in retention, and his division scored an overall employee satisfaction rating of 4.37 out of a possible 5.00. Lee's management concepts are simple (and strikingly familiar).

- Help the organization succeed by getting everyone on board with meaningful goals and then rewards for achievement.

- Maintain an open and consultative communication style that provides an environment where employees have the opportunity to do what they do best every day.

- Build trust by being ever vigilant to "find someone in the act of caring," and then share the credit by recognizing this person publicly and in a timely manner.

- Believe that people can create and succeed, and hold them accountable for great results.

For Elliot and others like him, the Carrot Principle has become second nature, and so has success. To help you put the Carrot Principle to work in your organization, the following pages are designed as a high-level primer, exploring the importance of the Basic Four both before and after we add the accelerator.

Setting Clear Goals

Sisyphus was a king in Greek mythology who offended the gods. His punishment was to roll an enormous boulder up a steep incline in Hades, only to watch it roll back down to the bottom of the hill, where he would begin the process again. It seems that the ancient Greek version of hell is much like the work life of many modern employees: a meaningless task with no end in sight. Too many companies are operating in a vacuum where employees and even their leaders have no idea what is valued. Deprived of direction, employees coast along, getting nowhere fast.

While leaders cannot often change the tasks in their organizations, they can change employees' attitudes toward their jobs by setting clear corporate or team goals. By defining the purpose of a task and tying it to a desirable end result, effective leaders infuse work with meaning and purpose. The task remains the same, but its significance in employees' minds skyrockets.

Let's take the health care industry as an example. Unlike most other industries, it benefits from having a fundamentally satisfying inherent goal: many people choose to work in this field because they want to help others feel better, and there are few more noble goals. Even so, health care organizations that produce the highest employee and customer satisfaction are shown to foster a strong sense of mission and purpose.

In one such system with more than sixty hospitals, leaders routinely offer a survey that asks employees whether "the mission and core values add meaning to my work." This system wove its goals and values into the recruiting process, employee evaluations, and strategic planning. Because it began to wrap the day-to-day life of the organization completely around its mission and values, it achieved a statistically significant jump in scores on this question from a ranking of thirty-fifth percentile nationally in 2002 to the sixty-first percentile in 2004.

But what happens if your mission is not as grandiose as that in health care? What if you manufacture rubber chickens? Fine. Just so the mission is clear (we suggest something like: "We create the most lifelike dead fowl in the world") and the goals are obtainable.

No matter what you sell or where you sell it, great managers in all industries infuse their employees' work with a clear sense of purpose. They not only explain the mission of the organization in terms of serving customers, acting with integrity, being the best in their industry, and so on, but how that grand, overarching mission applies to specific goals for their team and each individual's daily work. Employees need clarity from their leaders: clarity of goals, clarity of progress, and clarity of success. Not only that, they need leaders who set an optimistic tone for the future.

A leader has to focus every day on gaining alignment with what matters most to the company. She has to notice and reward the good things and quickly take action when employees do not act in accordance with mission or values. Any way you look at it, that's hard work.

Surprisingly, many leaders think their job of pursuing a central goal ends once the company values are written. "We printed wallet cards; everybody got one. And we've made sure each conference room has a framed poster with the values," a leader once told us. Then the leaders seem surprised when people's behavior does not conform to the organization's stated values.

The large hospital system we mentioned earlier also hardwires its core values into everything it does. It makes a difference. Because the system believes, "You are what you measure," they ask employees to rate the organization on this statement: "The hospital demonstrates its core values through its decisions and policies." It is no coincidence that overall employee satisfaction rose from the fifty-fifth percentile nationally to the seventy-fourth percentile in just two years.

We've found that while goal setting may seem to be a basic management skill, it is actually rare to find a manager who does this effectively. Here's one example. Now and then we are asked to consult with sales groups on effective motivation and are always surprised when we find so many regional offices that have little more than a vague overall sales quota from headquarters. The salespeople often have no organized plan to hit that quota, have not been led to identify the key prospects in their area, have not considered how they might mine more business out of current customers by identifying product needs, and so on. In short, the high-level quota has not been translated to daily individual goals for the salespeople.

Think back to the best managers you've had. Chances are, they not only helped you understand where you were going as a team, but where you could go as an individual to benefit your career. Great managers help interconnect an employee's goals and the company's goals. That interconnection is leadership, and when it happens, it's remarkable.

In fact, the power of a clearly communicated goal is so amazing that legends center around it. Almost all cultures have created myths about epic journeys through danger, despair, and, ultimately, triumph. Inevitably, what makes the journey and its trials worthwhile is the hero's noble purpose—his or her goal (which, we might add, is almost always achieved). In fact, in our research, we found that goal setting had a stronger correlation to employee satisfaction than the other Basic Four skills.

Gary, a bright young man we met at a recent training session, certainly recognized the power of goal setting. He explained how he had worked for an organization for almost ten years. But don't ask him what senior management was thinking: "I'm certain we had a mission statement and a codified list of goals, but in all my time there, I can't recall a single word being said about them. Everything was passive. Senior management never showed us what our goals were or what our mission was." He quipped, "That's like not knowing your girlfriend's a vegetarian or a Republican. You are bound to make mistakes."

Compare that with his current job: "My supervisor is fanatical about our mission and goals. I am surrounded by colleagues who can recite our mission and goals in their sleep. It's in the water we drink and the air we breathe. That internalized knowledge helps us not only handle the big decisions, but the day-to-day details as well. Most important of all, though, is that he walks his talk and he praises all who do the same. *Mission* is where you are going and *goals* get you there. More leaders should start seeing *mission* and *goals* as verbs, not nouns."

As excellence is constantly redefined in virtually every industry, goal setting is absolutely critical to staying ahead of the competition. Having challenging (yet attainable) goals provides the framework for continued success.

There are few challenges like the notoriously chaotic and unpredictable environment of a hospital emergency department. Dr. Gail Cunningham of St. Joseph Medical Center of Maryland (a case study from The Jackson Organization) illuminates the concept of good management in this setting: "We found that just by setting goals, the staff responded by meeting and exceeding them. Before, we weren't tracking 'door to provider' time, for example, but as soon as we set a time target, everyone became aware of the time. Now, if anyone sees a patient on the board getting close to the time limit, they spring into action."

Communicating Openly

In the early 1990s, we read an employee publication of an energy company in the Rocky Mountains. The new CEO disclosed that he believed in a "need-to-know" policy of communicating with employees. He went on to say that giving employees any information that was not specific to their jobs was distracting and a waste of time. We grimaced, as we are sure most of his employees did. It was obvious this one guy would decide who needed to know what in that organization. It was also clear that the CEO didn't think opening the conversation up to workers would spark any more ideas than he could generate himself.

We guessed he would last twelve months. He actually lasted less. By the time he left, the energy concern was in shambles.

Interestingly, in a recent survey by Right Management Consultants of employees in 336 organizations, only one-third of employees know or understand their employer's business strategy. That might not sound like a big deal at first, but not knowing, being left out of the loop, was the single biggest cause of dissatisfaction among the employees surveyed. It turns out employees have good reason to complain. Some 67 percent of the organizations surveyed either (1) limit communication of business strategies to their leadership teams, (2) have not yet gotten around to communicating to employees, or (3) don't know how to spread the word in an understandable, effective manner. Is there any question that our grand strategies never get executed?

A senior leader's job isn't to have all the ideas or even most of them. Her job is to communicate corporate goals to employees and motivate them to achieve them. The same applies to a manager. That is a paradigm shift for many of us, requiring a level of trust in employee abilities.

Jack Welch, retired CEO of General Electric, explained it well when he said, "I think any company . . . has got to find a way to engage the mind of every single employee. . . . If you're not thinking all the time about making every person more valuable, you don't have a chance. What is the alternative? Wasted minds? Uninvolved people? A labor force that's angry or bored? That doesn't make sense."

When you stop to think about it, communication within an organization is going to happen with or without a leader's active participation. Communication is happening every day among employees. They are talking about the computers or their tools, the company, supervisors, other employees, benefits, parking spaces, processes, rules, office romances, the bad coffee—you name it. If it exists in a corporation, someone, somewhere, is talking about it. So when a leader fails to constantly and openly communicate "who we are and what's important," the conversation doesn't stop. The dialogue among employees just goes in a different direction, and the company culture develops away from the leader's influence, goals, and priorities.

A leader who communicates openly with employees typically uses less authority and coercion to keep the company on track. As Dwight D. Eisenhower once said, "You do not lead by hitting people over the head—that's assault, not leadership."

So what do leaders who openly communicate do? For starters, they:

- Set clear guiding values and goals.

- Discuss issues facing the company and the team—not just the big decisions and announcements.

- Pass on all useful bits of information to employees, especially those that involve change initiatives or that personally affect employees.

- Make time for employees and listen intently when they express opinions and concerns.

- Welcome open discussion from team members about rumors they hear.

- Respond promptly to team member requests for more information.

- Go up their own chain of command to fill in the details they don't know.

- Introduce employees to other key individuals in the organization, sparking dialogue.

- Give employees online access to relevant databases.

Of course, leaders communicate on many other levels as well. They communicate by example, gesture, their decisions, what they value and what they celebrate, what they reward and what they don't reward, and their actions.

But one thing they can't do is communicate from their offices.

Sure, the meetings, conference calls, and reports are all important. But the things that keep us in our offices are nowhere near as important as open communication with employees. As Bill George, former chairman and CEO of Medtronic, explained, "Too many leaders . . . occupy themselves too much with things and don't pay enough attention to their people. They do so at their peril, because their employees interpret them and respond accordingly—in a compliant fashion rather than with their best work."

And you need their best work. At a time when productivity and creativity are more important than ever before, a company cannot afford lukewarm employees. More to the point, a company cannot afford leaders who can't lead and managers who can't manage. Lead what? Not projects. Manage what? Not a spreadsheet.

But people. And it's impossible to manage people without open communication. Opening up communication literally opens the door to success for you, your employees, and your company.

Take the example of shipping giant DHL, the world's largest express carrier. A few years ago, DHL realized it needed to do something remarkable to solidify its position and gain market share in the United States, where it was a distant third. It decided to focus on "Legendary Customer Service" as a core strategy, and then introduced the "I'm On It" advertising campaign. With the right strategy and the right marketing campaign, the firm realized that would be effective only if employees lived that brand of exceptional customer service, so it got everybody involved.

"While we have a directive from corporate, every department and every region has a voice in setting their own goals," said Scott Northcutt, global executive vice president of human resources for DHL. "Getting employees involved ensures that every driver, manager, and employee understands the goal, is accountable for the outcomes, and shares in the successes. Without our 'I'm On It' communication and challenging goals, we wouldn't be where we are today."

DHL today is enjoying vastly improved name recognition and a resulting upswing in revenue from U.S. operations. As for where it wants to be in the future, for managers at DHL—and everywhere else in the world—open communication is a key to achieving goals and becoming an industry leader.

Building Trust

Trust is often viewed as more of an interpersonal quality than a leadership skill. That's a mistake, since it turns out that trust is such a central concept in business that it can actually affect a country's economic growth. Paul Zak, professor of economics at Claremont University, has found that within a society, trust encourages investment and reduces the transaction costs associated with doing business. In a society where less than 30 percent of people trust each other, poverty typically increases.

The same can be said for a business or a team. In an organization where leaders are trusted, there is a greater level of employee investment. When an employee believes a manager has his best interest at heart, it motivates him to give his best to his work and the company, which creates higher overall commitment and that equals improved profitability. That's what Watson Wyatt Worldwide found when it surveyed 7,500 workers. Firms with high-commitment employees reported a three-year total return to shareholders 50 percent higher than in organizations where employees reported low commitment.

Louis Barnes, professor emeritus at Harvard Business School, describes the trust phenomenon as the theory of reciprocity: in short, people respond in kind to the way they are treated. For managers who want to build trust within the organization, this means respecting and listening to employees, treating them fairly, and worrying about the success of their team more than their own success. A leader who is trusted displays the following characteristics:

- Publicly owning up to his mistakes

- Keeping her word and commitments

- Surrounding himself with people who can be trusted

- Consistently taking the high road in ethically gray areas

- Refusing to participate in any level of deception

- Actively contributing to the positive reputation of the firm

It's an impressive list of qualities, perhaps maybe even a little bit intimidating for many of us. We've found that a good place for leaders to start the process of building trust is by becoming more visible to employees. Our experience has shown that getting out of the office and mingling with employees is a simple solution to a very common trust problem. In conducting organizational improvement workshops, we routinely ask, "What is the single greatest barrier to improving communication and trust between you and your manager?" In nearly every case, the first response is, "I never see her. She's always in a meeting."

This was the problem at one East Coast organization where an employee survey revealed low trust scores for senior leaders. In follow-up focus groups, it was learned that the CEO seldom ventured far from the office, choosing to communicate through e-mail. A frequent comment was, "He arrives every morning in his limo, goes to the fourth floor, and we never see him." The employees could not develop a perception of trust with higher-ups when some didn't even know who the CEO was. Despite recommendations to change, the CEO stayed in the office. He is no longer a part of that organization.

With leaders like this, it's no wonder that only half of the workers polled in the Watson Wyatt Worldwide survey said they were committed to their employer, and fewer than half said they had confidence in management. But there is hope. Another firm we worked with in the southern United States experienced similarly low trust scores on its first survey. However, the CEO took ownership of the finding and began holding "town hall meetings," which were essentially brown-bag lunches where employees could talk with the president. He also required all vice presidents to visit with workers in and outside their own departments. The result was not only higher trust scores in the second survey but greater employee satisfaction.

This company's experience is not unique. While trust is a complex issue that we are simplifying to one solution, trusting relationships with employees can begin with leaders' being more visible and available. It's a place to start—something that will be noticed and appreciated by the people in your care.

Holding People Accountable

CACI, a leading information technology firm with 10,000 employees, could write the book on creating corporate culture. So a few years ago, it did—for its employees.

Illustrated with engaging original artwork and honest writing, the book included the following section on accountability, written to CACI employees by the chairman of the board, CEO, and president, Dr. J. P. (Jack) London:

At CACI, we hold ourselves accountable for being honest in all our dealings. We don't make excuses; we make it RIGHT.

Of course, that doesn't mean that we never make mistakes. Every organization does. And we are no different. We know we are not perfect, and we take ownership when we are in error. (After all, if you can't admit a mistake, you certainly can't fix it.) Then we correct our mistakes, and we correct them quickly. We do this even when it hurts.

When it comes right down to it, accountability means that if you or I make a promise to a client, we fulfill that promise. We make every effort to ensure that the client receives exactly what they expected to get, as a result of our agreement. And we don't just do this because it's on paper. We do it because it's the right thing to do and because it is just good business.

CACI's commitment to accountability is demonstrated in its Excellence+ program, which measures customer satisfaction. In this program, the technology firm uses self-assessments, customer surveys, and third-party evaluations to obtain candid feedback from all of its clients, partners, subcontractors, and vendors. If it finds any areas that do not meet CACI or the customer's desired standard, project leaders pledge to fix the problem within ninety days. In reality, most problems are corrected within thirty days because, like most other accountable organizations, CACI can't stand to have something out of kilter.

"CACI has worked tirelessly through the years to build a reputation of accountability. As a result, because CACI people are known to be accountable for their work, clients want CACI products, industry partners want to work with us, and individuals want to be employed by us," said London. Across the United States and across the rest of the world, the CACI name is a good and honorable name. And continued accountability is one way they make sure it stays that way.

That's about the most straightforward explanation of accountability we've ever heard.

If we had to pick one key to holding people accountable and doing it right, we would say it's equilibrium. As a leader, you must develop the ability to identify not only employee failures, but a greater percentage of employee successes. And that can be a difficult balancing act. One employee we interviewed in the hotel industry brought this concept to life for us when she said, "When I make a mistake I'm recognized 100 percent of the time; when I do something great, I'm not recognized 99 percent of the time."

Of course, that's a mistake in and of itself. Some of the greatest leaders have come to realize that the line between mistakes and failures can be very thin. Many well-known organizations have developed awards for intelligent mistakes. They realize that in an atmosphere of speed and innovation, workers need to feel safe to adapt, innovate, and experiment. That means, of course, that some mistakes will be made—and that's all right. In these cultures, part of holding people accountable is celebrating mistakes that were worth being made.

Sales consultant and best-selling author Jeffrey Gitomer has introduced an interesting tactic to celebrate mistakes with his team of employees. He rewards his people with a crisp $100 bill when they admit a mistake. "I'll often have people walk in and say, 'Jeffrey, I need a bonus. I really screwed up.' That's fine with me. I want them to know that they can take risks—that they don't need to be perfect."

Of course, in a culture with equilibrium, there is a great focus on celebrating successes. Recognition is frequent and meaningful and reinforces the notion of accountability. And what's poignant in these cultures is that great managers don't just hold their people accountable in formal ways. In many cases, you might not even know you're being held accountable. You just know you don't want to let that manager down.

An advertising executive we interviewed recounted the story of his first boss. A pending audit had caught them unprepared, and she asked him to inventory all the computer equipment in the office. It was outside his job scope, and a little entry level for his tastes. But he respected the manager and didn't want to let her down. So that night he stayed late and tallied everything. By the next morning, the list was on her desk.

We'd say that manager was skilled in holding people accountable without having to use the whip. This ad guy didn't really think of that. He just said she was a great boss and he would have hated to disappoint her. For us, that really says it all.

Goal setting, communication, trust, and accountability. Our research, validated by The Jackson Organization's study, has shown these are the Basic Four of effective management. Alone, each one can move you quite a way toward business results, but when a manager is even somewhat competent with the Basic Four and then adds the accelerator to each, management effectiveness soars. In the next chapter we'll show you how that works.

3

Leadership Accelerated

To each of the Basic Four of leadership, the application of the Carrot Principle is a powerful accelerant. The ways in which recognition reinforces these other characteristics of good management range from the obvious to the surprising.

Goal Setting *Accelerated*

One of the powerful ways that recognition reinforces goal setting is that the act of rewarding activities that move employees closer to the goal allows leaders to correct the group's course in a positive way rather than pointing out deficiencies in performance. Research by Edward L. Deci and his colleagues shows that positive feedback increases the sense of competence, while negative feedback undermines it.

Leadership gurus Kouzes and Posner describe the impact of individual recognition on the work group this way: "By lifting the spirits of people [through recognition and celebration], we heighten awareness of organization expectations and humanize the values and standards such that we motivate at a deep and enduring level. But even more, public recognition serves as a valuable educational mechanism demonstrating company values and encouraging others to duplicate the actions they see rewarded."

Recognition further accelerates progress toward a goal by bringing new energy to its pursuit. While communicating a clear goal and purpose may be enough for employees to begin a task with enthusiasm, people must feel that they are making progress, or their enthusiasm will begin to wane. Since we were children, we've asked, "Are we there yet?" As we grow into adults, we typically become more patient, but the need to hit milestones doesn't diminish. "The childhood need to 'be there now' evolves into the need to feel that you are getting there—that you are making progress," says motivation writer Kenneth Thomas. Workplace recognition weds our adult reasoning skills with our childlike enthusiasm, creating a perfect union of employee involvement.

That is a great description of what has occurred at Minneapolis-based Xcel Energy, where a core goal has been to innovate and improve. The company realized this value would be achieved only by enlisting the help of all 10,000 employees. The result has been thousands of improvements to systems, processes, and working conditions that equaled $17 million in savings opportunities. In true accelerator form, the quest of this leading energy provider to turn problems into improvements is spurred by the company's Xpress Ideas suggestion recognition program. And, says the program's executive sponsor, Bill Newby, "Our investment in recognition is earning our company at least a twenty-times return."

Xcel Energy has never underestimated the power of targeted, strategic recognition. The company uses several types of recognition programs to encourage employee engagement, involvement, and ownership in the company. And it even offers managers recognition consulting services through its Corporate Rewards and Recognition Team. The team meets with business units to discover recognition approaches that will target specific goals and problems. For example, if it's a cash crunch, they'll find a way to recognize those who save money. If they are having safety issues, they want to promote recognition for those who improve safety conditions.

John Torres is manager of corporate rewards and recognition, a job created by Xcel Energy to maximize its recognition investment. He observes, "The managers welcome our help because they see results. They're not just looking at the program as, 'I have to write another thank-you note.' They're looking at it as, 'This helps me encourage employees to improve business results.' That's something they get to report to their boss. It motivates everyone in the process."

With the suggestion program, the firm wanted to implement a corporatewide system to not only make this core goal more relevant to employees, but to elevate the caliber of managers. Thus, Xcel Energy invested in making its employee suggestion recognition program more strategic. The program was designed to be more than just a way of rewarding effort: Xcel Energy created recognition systems that become a way for managers to begin conversations about improvement with employees—tools that inspire thought, action, and results.

The first step was to get managers behind the program, and that meant streamlining processes. The company has put its application online and has given every manager the systems, technology, and tools to make recognition simple and more easily measured.

Now, we've all tried the infamous suggestion box. Along with gum wrappers, crumpled-up sticky notes, and ideas such as, "I suggest you pay me more," these boxes typically add nothing to our bottom lines. At Xcel, the result has been 13,000 ideas in the past two years. What struck us was not only that the quantity of suggestions has increased with the application of the accelerator, but the quality of suggestions was also enhanced. The fact that two-thirds of the ideas were implemented is a testament to their efficacy.

"I have managers who tell me their employees used to come

to work asking, 'How do I do a good job today?' Now they ask, 'How do I do it better?'" said Torres.

As companies like Xcel Energy show us, it's almost impossible to strategically reward employees if you don't set clear goals. Chances are that without clearly outlining target goals, you'd only be rewarding actions that are outside the job scope, sending the wrong messages.

Communication *Accelerated*

Let's say you have something extremely important to share with your employees—information they can't do without. How will you communicate it? We asked this question recently to a group of senior business executives. A woman raised her hand (perhaps she was the director of communication) and said, "We'd put it in the company newsletter."

"Okay," we said. "Now what if you wanted everyone to actually find out about it?"

A sardonic chuckle broke out among the group. A man, perhaps in information technology, hazarded a guess: "Send them to our intranet."

"Yes, and some people would go there," we said. "But what next level would you go to if they just *had* to find out about it?"

"An e-mail blast," said another.

"No, we'd have an all-hands company meeting," shouted out another.

"It'd be better to have a department meeting," argued a voice.

We nodded and asked, "But could you be sure that everyone would pay attention during the meeting, and every single person would leave with the message in the way you had intended it? What if you really, *really* wanted your employees to learn about something?"

"I'd tell them in person. One on one," said a savvy woman near the front.

"Bingo."

The assumption of many managers is that important information will come from the head office or human resources. But when we push a little harder, a manager's intuition tells them that if they have something important to share, they do it in person, one by one. Chances are that in this case, if what you had to communicate was *that* important, you might even go to the employee's home to share the news.

Here's what it boils down to:

> We communicate with the masses,
> but we manage to the one.

As managers, we rely on the organization to send out newsletters, videos, and posters. We have company meetings and give speeches to rally the troops. We have attractive intranet sites with Flash animation. We hang inspirational posters touting our values and send out news-filled e-mails. But while all that information may be helpful to a few select souls, very little of that communication really changes employee behavior. That's why great leaders realize they must manage to the one.

Of course, most of us know that those messages to the masses are important in setting a tone and reinforcing the work employees do. We may also know that statistics show that company information in written, electronic, or video form is important to future leaders of the company who are readers by nature and seek out all the information they can lay their hands on. And we may also acknowledge the legal and moral ramifications of trying to share as many important messages as possible.

But effective managers also realize that to influence behavior, to explain what really matters most, they must speak to each individual in their charge frequently, specifically, and in a timely manner. The most effective way to do that is through employee recognition.

Here's why. Although you may think you speak the same language as your employees, you might be surprised. Mission.

Company values. Goals. It's all Greek to the majority of workers. Don't get us wrong; they're not stupid. They're just not very interested in what leaders have to say.

Recognition, however, is a universal translator that can convert high-level goals into clear, everyday activities that employees can easily get behind and move forward. Take, as an example, a floor supervisor who observes an employee in a hardware store not just pointing out that dryer hoses are located on aisle four, but taking the time to escort the customer there, find the right equipment, and explain proper installation.

The leader stops the employee a few moments later. "Ron, that was a perfect example of our value 'service that makes them smile.' I know you were busy stocking, but you walked that customer right over to the right aisle and you did it with a smile on your face. You went above and beyond in helping her. Why don't you take these movie tickets and take your girlfriend out to a show this weekend with our thanks."

This is a fictional example, but we hope it conveys the message. Personalized recognition like this gets everyone's attention. It's something everyone understands. In those few seconds, the leader communicated to this employee in an unforgettable way what is important at this store.

Even better, assume the leader had done this in a group. Employees watching such a presentation would think, "I want to do that next time." Would that be more strategic than your last memo on customer service or the "Put the Client First" banner over everyone's heads in the break room? Of course.

And as this example illustrates, recognition doesn't have to be a long, drawn-out affair. It can take just a few seconds, debunking the popular manager excuse that they don't have time to recognize.

Leaders who have made the connection between recognition and communication soon discover that employees are making all sorts of connections—not just mentally, but behaviorally, and even emotionally.

Message Sent by Manager	Message Received by Employee
"I saw how you helped that customer . . ."	*My boss notices what I do.*
"This is a perfect example of our value of . . ."	*I belong to a firm worth working for.*
"We have another reason to celebrate as a team . . ."	*We are winners, and we are winning.*
"This really is one of your strong points . . ."	*I have pride in my work and can do even better.*
"I know you can accomplish this . . ."	*I can do this and will be rewarded for my hard work.*
"I'd like to thank you for five years of extraordinary . . ."	*This is where I belong.*
"Thanks for staying late to get that out . . ."	*I'll do anything to help the team succeed.*

Kent Murdock, O. C. Tanner Company CEO, explained the communicative power of recognition this way: "For example, in a recognition celebration where we gather peers and supervisors, a recipient in our manufacturing group might be commended for 'dependability,' which in a manufacturing cell is the highest virtue. She might also be noted by her peers for 'helping everyone learn the new system,' or for 'pitching in and helping with a problem that wasn't her responsibility,' or even for 'innovating to save us time and money.' Recognition could come for 'doing anything it takes to satisfy the customer,' or for 'skipping break or staying late to make sure the order went out,' or for 'taking on the most difficult jobs,' or for 'being a real hard worker, always dedicated.'

"I have heard every one of those comments in recognition gatherings in the last week or two in our firm. If that kind of communication is going on in a company day by day or week by week, there is an almost constant reinforcement of company values, productive workplace behaviors, and cultural norms. Everyone observing the recognition experience is drawn into the same reinforcing communication. The impact far surpasses anything I could have accomplished through a speech. These are truly the best speeches a corporate leader *never* gave."

Because recognition holds employee interest so well, no one tunes out when you are giving an award—not the employee being recognized and certainly not those in attendance who are wondering what they need to do to be the next person recognized.

Recognition is effective because it answers a universal human need. We all want to matter to those with whom we work. Communication combined with recognition of strategically important behaviors takes your vision and values off the wall and puts them into the hearts and minds of your people, which is exactly the place you want your vision and values to be.

Trust *Accelerated*

The moment you publicly recognize someone for a contribution, the trust meter shoots off the scale. In that moment, the employee being recognized, and everyone present for the celebration, realizes they can trust you to share the credit. They realize you are not going to hog the spotlight. It becomes abundantly clear that you are a team player who values others.

"This innate need for appreciation is not a selfish, superficial craving for the center spotlight; it is an authentic, deep-seated desire to be deemed as worthy when offering something of worth," said Deal and Key in their book *Corporate Celebration*.

The frequent act of recognition also bonds individual team members to you and each other. A specific, sincere compliment reaches employees on an emotional level that no other form of business communication can. It is at once extremely professional and incredibly personal. The results of this acceleration are closer employee-manager relationships, greater respect, and a sense of fairness in your team. Follow the chain a little further, and you'll find that the result of this kind of an accelerated team relationship is greater productivity. It's a simple concept: we all work harder for people we like and respect, and we like and respect people who show a certain regard for us. As British industrialist John Ashcroft once said, "The worst mistake a boss can make is not to say 'well done.'"

Well, maybe not the worst. Don't get us wrong; failing to recognize is a significant mistake. But there's another. Like you, we've seen enough really horrible award presentations to realize that when recognition is done poorly, it can also hurt trust. Imagine being gathered together and your manager saying, "I just got an award from corporate for Mike. What did you do, Mike? Oh, yeah. That new freight consolidation system. I even bailed you out when that project was going badly. Well, I wish I had one of these awards for everyone here. Everyone works really hard. I know that."

Do you think Mike will ever go above and beyond again? How about those in attendance?

Contrast that type of recognition with what occurred recently in an Arizona sales department meeting room at 2:30 A.M. under bright fluorescent lights. The morning delivery shift of the Phoenix area Pepsi Bottling Group (PBG) was about to head out, and bulk delivery supervisor Henry Patton was giving some last-minute instructions to his people. Before they broke, Henry used simple recognition to great effect. It could have been a sales award he was presenting, or a safety award, or an above-and-beyond award. But in this case, it was Roger Carey's fifteenth anniversary with PBG, and Henry realized that deserved public recognition.

At first glance, you might think these PBG drivers are a pretty irreverent crowd. They sit in their blue work shirts around a horseshoe of nondescript tables, firing back jabs at Henry as he leads them through the day's instructions. As for Henry, he seems about as menacing as a six-foot teddy bear. But

looks can be deceiving. Although the employees may seem dis-
connected, they are anything but. They are listening and engaged. They care about the success of PBG, their team, and each
other. And Henry is allowing the banter with good humor and
some jabs back as he meticulously finishes his instructions: setting clear goals, communicating openly, holding the team accountable, and building the trust of everyone in the room.

We'll join the discussion as Henry uses recognition to accelerate all he has done:

*Henry: I want to finish our meeting today with some well-
deserved recognition. This person came to the Pepsi Bottling
Group fifteen years ago looking for a good career. He's taken on
a lot of challenges in that time. That person is Roger
Carey . . . outstanding citizen.* (Laughter from the group. Ribbing.) *I know he doesn't like to be in the spotlight much, so
we'll keep it short. In his fifteen years, Rog has been in full-
service vending; that's where he started. Then he decided to be a
sales rep for a while. Then he brought all that experience over
here to bulk delivery and has been enjoying that ever since.
Come on up here, Roger, I've got a nice award for you.* (Clap-
ping from group as Roger comes up to the front to shake
Henry's hand. The ribbing stops as if on cue.) *Fifteen years,
Roger. That deserves our congratulations. You know, one thing
I like about Roger: no matter what we ask him to do, he's there
to help us out. He lives the Pepsi Bottling Group philosophy of
Act Now, Do It Today, and Get Results. Let me give just one
example. Roger will often call me from an account when he's
found something loaded improperly—say, he has a pallet of
twelve-pack cans on the truck and the sales rep ordered two-
liter bottles. Sometimes we can send out the right product, but if
it's too late, Roger doesn't hesitate in coming back here to get
the right product and taking it back out to the store so there are
no lost sales or revenues, not to mention upset customers and
store managers.*

The great thing about Roger is that he's committed to doing

whatever it takes so that our stores have the right product the same day so there's no out-of-stock situation.
  Roger: Thanks, Henry.
  Henry: Does anyone else have anything to say about Roger?
(A vociferous return to the laughter and joking for a few moments. After the room quiets, employees add their thoughts on Roger. Here's just one:)
  Coworker: I'd like to thank Roger. I was coming from full-service, and he made my transition a lot smoother. I was struggling. I'd never done sales. And he made my transition a lot easier. I really appreciate that.
  Henry: Yeah. We do appreciate you, Roger. If every plant in this company had a Roger Carey, we'd be doing just outstanding. So once again, thanks, Rog.

Think about what just happened in this example. First, Henry appreciated the wealth of experience Roger had brought from other departments to his role in bulk delivery. Next, he talked about Roger's dependability and how he lived the Pepsi Bottling Group values of Act Now, Do It Today, and Get Results. He told a poignant but brief story about Roger and how he lived those values: doing whatever it took after a system error to get the right product to the right store on the right day. Next, Henry didn't hog the spotlight, but allowed other employees to speak up. One talked about Roger's role in teamwork, another PBG value. And finally, Henry gave him a great compliment: that if every department had a Roger Carey, the Pepsi Bottling Group would be even stronger than it is today.

Does Roger feel more engaged after that two-minute exchange? Of course. Does everyone in attendance know what Henry values? Act Now, Do It Today, Get Results; teamwork; dependability; and loyalty are all important at PBG.

And finally, Henry is more trusted because of this simple exchange. He values the people in his charge and notices the unique skills they bring to the organization. He's not afraid to hear what other employees think. He's willing and happy to take the time—in a very busy day, with thirty direct reports, and pressing customer demands to hit the road—to single out an employee for exemplary behavior.

It's part of an overarching business strategy at this company that includes creative and all-encompassing recognition efforts. In fact, recognition begins from day one at PBG as each new employee receives a welcome award. Along the way, employees can be recognized on the company's online Wall of Fame, and even spouses can be recognized with a beautiful silver clock. The CEO gets involved by signing a personalized letter to all employees who celebrate thirty-five years or more with the company. And finally, at retirement, PBG commemorates departing employees in style with a selection of appropriate awards.

With the right tools, PBG managers like Henry Patton are using recognition to accelerate trust in their organization.

Accountability *Accelerated*

The other day, after witnessing a mild disciplinary moment between some parents and their son in the grocery store, one of us watched as the wife turned to her husband and asked, half in jest, "Why is he *my* son every time he does something wrong, but *our* son the rest of the time?"

We laughed, but had to admit she was right. Too often, we treat accountability as a negative. But when you add recognition to the equation, it can be extremely positive.

Think of it this way. As a manager, you typically would not wait until the end of a project to receive an update from your people, but will check on their progress along the way. By recognizing accomplishments and the milestones toward larger goals, you let employees know in a positive way that they're being held accountable for the overall success of the project.

To hold your people accountable, give recognition whenever an employee delivers, especially when he or she does so in an above-and-beyond manner. Why? Because if you don't recognize them, there's a very good chance they might not deliver again, especially if it takes extra effort, time, or stress. Conversely, when you *do* recognize, it accelerates engagement because employees know their accomplishments will be noticed and rewarded. Recognition is a very visible, very positive way to hold employees accountable. After all, if you are going to hold employees accountable for their shortcomings, you must also hold them accountable for their achievements. It's the right thing to do. It's the fair thing to do.

That feeling of accountability can be enhanced when a visible recognition award is given. Each time the employee sees the award, it will trigger the feeling of accountability for a project's success, building personal pride and commitment, and acting as an accelerator as the person moves toward a new goal.

4

Altruists and Expectors

We wouldn't blame you if, based on your experience, you had doubts about the power of recognition. Like us, you have probably seen your share of bad recognition: awful business trinkets or walnut plaques presented to employees with the idea of changing behavior. We have witnessed the presentation of a mountain of plastic mugs, have sat through an endless parade of dull year-end banquets, and have glanced at millions of inspirational posters plastered over the unsuspecting walls of corporate America.

Looking on, we have often wished motivating employees was really that easy. Imagine overhearing this conversation on the elevator one morning between your CEO and his chief lieutenant:

CEO: What's happening in Baltimore? Revenue there is up 20 percent!

VP: You know, I'm not sure. But I did put up a poster there last month—the one with the rowers all pulling in the same direction.

CEO: *Ah, yes. That's one of my favorites. Well, put up twice as many posters, and double everyone's quotas.*

If it were really that simple, even this approach could have some interesting consequences. A few months down the line, you might overhear the two again:

CEO: *What's up with Philadelphia? They haven't been motivated at all by the posters.*
VP: *Yeah, we have a problem there. No wall space.*

Recognition done well encompasses much more than inspirational wall hangings, logoed hats, or the other trappings that managers and organizations often turn to. Effective recognition is a little hard (but worthwhile). It's strategic. It's timely. It's frequent. But most important, it's human.

The Groupings from the Research

For our purposes, managers can be grouped into two general categories: recognition practitioners (believers and users) and nonrecognition practitioners (which include those doing no recognition and those managers doing very little). That second group accounts for the majority of managers. A recent Gallup Poll found that 65 percent of Americans received no praise or recognition in the workplace in the past year. It's an abysmal statistic, most likely brought on because so few organizations give their managers the tools and training they need to provide recognition to their people.

As we worked more closely with the group of managers who *were* practicing some form of recognition, we found a curious distinction in their ranks. We found a large group of recognizing managers who hand out recognition awards—say, a pair of movie tickets—but they *expect* something in return. We called this group of managers the Expectors.

These managers may offer up a small recognition award but

expect, for example, that their employees will work the next weekend when asked. "When I need someone on short notice, I want them to be there," said one busy Expector. Another said, "I want that person to work hard for me when I go ask them to do something the next time." Frankly, it's hard to blame these folks for their approach. After all, they have pressures and deadlines, and they need the support of their people.

As we delved deeper into this group of Expectors in our focus groups and interviews, we discovered that most saw recognition as a necessary means to do business. In other words, they felt a need to acknowledge the contributions of individuals and teams. But the need was most often linked to the extreme pressure they felt to deliver corporate performance. They saw the cycle this way:

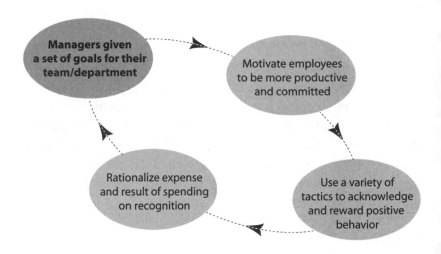

For many Expector managers, recognition efforts are linked to performance demands. They are given ever-increasing goals. Thus, recognition (often inadvertently) becomes a form of manipulation to drive productivity and loyalty among their employees and a means to relieve pressure on the manager by gaining the support of his people. To motivate, many of these managers realize it's their unspoken responsibility to come up with their own employee rewards for positive behavior. Since these managers approach recognition with themselves—rather than their employees—in mind, they look for quick and easy awards requiring little thought or preparation, often settling for one-size-fits-all rewards. Everyone gets a video rental certificate, a coffee card, a small cash bonus, an event ticket, or the same candy bar. Said one of these Expectors to us, "If you give a bag of M&Ms, always put a bow around it," as if that magically personalizes the reward.

Ironically, this type of recognition isn't cheap. Expector managers are routinely spending hundreds of dollars every year for on-the-spot awards. The median we found was $100 to $200 per employee annually. And they must rationalize, hide, or plead for reimbursement of the expense of their recognition efforts. Like public schoolteachers supplying their classrooms, some of these managers even admit funding the recognition activities out of their own pockets.

Yet despite this spending, when we asked these Expectors if they thought they were doing too much recognition, only one (a manager in a start-up tech company) said he was doing too much. Except for that fellow, the rest thought they needed to praise and reward more—with one caveat: Expectors worried that if they did give a lot more recognition, it would "lose meaning" or "lessen the impact," a variation on the "too many presents make spoiled kids" philosophy.

With all this confusion and stress, it's no wonder that most of the Expector managers we interviewed rarely linked recognition to a positive emotion. In fact, when we began speaking about this subject, the energy visibly drained from many, and most seemed to put on stiff corporate faces. They spoke about how recognition increased dependability, helped them hit company goals, enhanced productivity, and so on, but they showed no excitement about the subject. The warmest comment during this phase was from an Expector manager who offered, "Happy employees are more productive employees," ironically without the slightest trace of a smile.

It wasn't until we moved the discussion to how recognition affected those in their charge that the Expectors' body language changed. Then, with only a few exceptions, these managers admitted that they liked to see the smiles on their employees' faces or how it made them feel good to hand out praise. Said one Expector manager in Seattle, "I do like to see that they know I care." Said another in New York, "I actually feel better about myself when I share the credit." Another manager in Texas added, "It's the same feeling I get when I donate to the food bank."

The employees who work for the Expectors seemed to appreciate the recognition sentiment from their bosses, notwithstanding their bosses' motives. All agreed that it was certainly better than getting no recognition. But when pressed, they admitted in hushed tones that their boss's one-size-fits-all recognition often denoted a lack of knowledge of their specific drivers and lacked any true feeling or motivational power. Said one employee of her boss, "When he recognizes, I think, 'And . . . ' I always feel like I'm being set up to take on something new."

Strikingly, this worry was not shared by the employees working for managers who were giving recognition with a more altruistic, human motive. We call this group of managers the Altruists.

For the leaders within this group, recognition seemed to fulfill a deep-seated need. While they too admitted they could offer more recognition, not a single Altruist thought they could give too much.

Overall, the Altruists we found cared instinctively about their employees as individuals and took the time to find out what motivated each. They also recognized more often and were prompter in celebrating great behavior, and that made their efforts vastly more authentic with employees and much more successful in spurring greater achievement.

One of these leaders, a fire chief in Dallas, is a perfect example. When he spoke of his people, he didn't call them "staff," "employees," "troops," or even his "team." They were his *posse*. He talked about "hanging with them," and he spoke of the trust that they shared when they went into a burning building together. When asked if he felt he could give his people too much recognition, he looked at us as if we had lost our minds: "These guys walk through fire for me. . . . I mean they *really* do," he said. "Do you think 'thanks' for them ever gets old?"

Like our fire chief, Altruist managers rarely refer to the people in their charge as "employees," "staff," or even "team members." Instead, they call them by name, or call them "individuals," "people," "teammates," or even "family." In addition, they are not afraid of sharing the credit with their people. Said one of these managers, "My people are everything in terms of our performance." Another said, "I brag about my people all the time." They thought of recognition as a way to make the employee feel good and look good to others.

These Altruists:

- Have a deeper understanding of and higher regard for the underlying human need for recognition in their team members.

- Are compelled to improve the overall lives of their employees and in turn reap greater loyalty, respect, and trust from their people.

- Are able to achieve better performance for the company than Expector managers and nonrecognizing managers, but that is secondary to their sensitivity toward the individuals in their charge.

- Are either driven internally or influenced by a senior leadership group that uniquely cares for their people and gives managers the tools to effectively recognize.

The research shows that it doesn't matter what age you are—we found Altruists who were boomers and Gen-X managers. Gender doesn't matter either. While we found a greater percentage of women in the Expector group, Altruists were split evenly between genders.

With the enhanced performance and employee engagement this skill brings, you might wonder if this type of altruistic leadership is learnable. The simple answer is yes. Evidence of the ability to learn altruistic leadership comes from the higher percentage of Altruist managers in organizations where senior management provided the support, training, and tools for managers to celebrate their employees' small and not-so-small successes.

But before we begin a journey to becoming an Altruist manager, it's essential to think about our employees and what they need to succeed. When it comes to success, you start by getting to know your people.

Work and Self-Image

We must admit that we began *The Carrot Principle* with a bias about recognition. As consultants for the oldest and largest provider of employee recognition solutions, we have worked with some of the world's most successful organizations and have seen the impact of employee reward programs done well. But by the time we were done with our studies, interviews, focus groups, and surveys, our perspective had changed considerably.

What we found is that a lot of employee work motivation is not as externally driven as we have all believed. A good share of an employee's attitude toward work is internally driven by a person's desire for autonomy and achievement. To help their employees reach their goals, today's enlightened, effective managers are changing the way they lead. They have learned to motivate by tapping into a person's hopes and attitudes around work. They help employees realize their potential.

As far back as the publication of Abraham Maslow's *Hierarchy of Needs*, we have understood that people first seek to fill their physiological and safety needs—food and shelter. If wages are competitive and people are showing up for work, then the food and shelter need is most likely being met. So employees move on to fill their love/belonging needs. When these are met, they focus on their esteem needs. What all this means is that employees first need to feel safe at work, that their paychecks will clear, that there's only the most remote chance that they will be let go next week, and that if they get sick, their benefit plan will get them back on their feet again. Second, they need to feel as if they belong, that they have a vital role in the success of a team or enterprise. And finally, they are looking to feel important and valued in their jobs. In short, employees are seeking validation from their leaders.

In a culture of recognition, people seek the next level: self-actualization. Of course, this is a boon to any organization, as employees seeking self-actualization are striving to excel, to reach their highest potential. This is the level of performance where workers are engaged and willing to give their best efforts to their work, creating mutual benefit for the organization and the individual.

In the place of Maslow's pyramid, imagine another, this time with equitable salary and benefits as the bottom rung. The next rung would be a positive work experience, or how people feel on the job. The next rung would be recognition, which leads finally to the top rung, a self-actualized workforce.

Recognition is the missing step that helps people reach upward toward self-actualization. But before we can achieve self-actualization, we need recognition to provide confirmation of achievement—proof that others believe in what we can do. After all, there is a reason we keep our old sports and academic trophies; the recognition is evidence that our achievements are not just in our heads, but are acknowledged and esteemed by our peers and superiors.

Managers who lead without effective recognition are synonymous with a ladder with a fragile rung. And in teams like that, even employees who want to be engaged often fall through the cracks and, before long, disappear.

Thus, an immediate supervisor is the nexus of success in employee engagement. But not just any manager. The new realization that comes out of our research relates to the characteristics of an effective manager.

This is a relatively recent phenomenon brought about by the changing perceptions of our workforce. To back up quite a bit, work was once seen as human penance for evil beginnings in the Garden of Eden. Over the years, as socioeconomic classes arose in society in the Middle Ages, work began to be seen as the curse of the poor. The wealthy in society did all they could to avoid labor, perhaps except for war, which was seen as noble. Eventually enlightened philosophers such as St. Thomas Aquinas and his contemporaries taught that work was important, especially if we used our surplus to help others. Their teachings influenced reformers such as Martin Luther, who explained that work was virtuous if we had integrity and were honest in our dealings with our fellow men. Later, as America and Canada expanded into new territories, work in contemporary society was described as a privilege of the free. Then, as we entered the 1900s, Henry Ford and other industrialists convinced us that work led to progress for our society and our families.

Throughout the twentieth century, many swings occurred in

our moods about work, all culminating in the very interesting decade of the 1990s, when many of us looked at work as a means to an early retirement with appreciating stock options, bulging 401(k) accounts, or big cash rewards from impending initial public offerings. Then came the startling realities of the dot-com crash and 9/11, which left many employees disillusioned, doubting the dream of the early out. Our jobs have again become a way to make a living.

Work is not as synonymous with self as it was even a decade ago. Quality leisure and family time have now become imperative to most employees we interviewed, while the vast majority describe their work as a necessity, and in many cases an unpleasant one.

One bright woman when asked about her future with her current employer told us, "I'll continue to work here as long as there's a fair exchange." Certainly that is not a concept that workers in the paternal '50s would have articulated, or even in the '90s when employees expected an appreciable return from their work. Indeed, workers of the early twenty-first century expect, at best, a fair return. And as a general rule, they are being disappointed.

Today, workers are spending more hours on the job than ever before. Faced with a shortage of good jobs, increased competition, demanding executives, outsourcing and offshoring, and continuous process improvement, many employees find themselves plugged into work at all hours through laptops, wireless connections, cell phones, and other digital devices. In fact, some 25 million U.S. workers today report working an average of more than 50 hours a week, with 40 percent of those workaholics logging more than 60 hours a week. An average American or Canadian worker puts in a full month of hours (160 to be precise) more each year than a generation ago, more than the citizens of any other Western/European country, and even longer hours than medieval peasants in servitude did.

Adding to worker discontent is the fact that pay has not kept pace with additional productivity demands from employers. But perhaps the greatest insult is the lack of job security. Employees see the hunters of our firms—the salespeople, the CEOs, the division heads—reaping ever-grander salaries, bonuses, and perks as droves of their coworkers are laid off—even people who worked hard and added value.

Laurie is a salaried employee we spoke with during an interview in Toronto. "I'm not a stranger to long hours in a crunch," she told us. "But this was different." Laurie's manager needed a specialized report, and she needed it yesterday. "This was a 160-hour project. That's a month's worth of work right there. Oh, and she didn't want me to stop doing anything I was already doing. I'm not *that* good. No one is," she said. The irony, for Laurie, was that the company had laid off five members of her staff just a few months earlier. She was one of the few survivors.

But her manager had said it would be worth her while to work double time and pull this one off. Laurie checked with her husband (promised a weekend trip to somewhere warm when it was done), kissed her four-year-old good-bye, and spent the next several weeks camped in her office, eating a lot of lousy take-out dinners. She completed the project in three weeks, putting in an incredible 300 hours, and saving the company at least $30,000 in outsourcing costs. And what did Laurie get for her trouble? Four hundred dollars was added into her next paycheck.

"I won't play the fool again," said Laurie, shaking her head.

Her story is just one of many of the kind we heard, adding up to less loyalty among workers than in past generations, combined with more insecurity, stress, and discontent. Today's employees are:

Insecure
• Working hard doesn't ensure success.

- They have no assurance of job stability, promotion, or pay increases.

Stressed

- They face pressure from "productivity" and increased competition.

- Insecurity fosters the idea that performance is never enough.

- They are working harder than ever before.

Discontent

- More than 50 percent of workers are dissatisfied.

- Less leisure time increases reliance on work for fulfillment.

- Intrusion of work into home life creates resentment.

- Employees feel a lack of empowerment.

Disloyal

- More employees today view work merely as a job.

- Employment is viewed as temporary, and employees are often on the lookout for better work.

What does all this mean for a manager? Basically, as working has become a means to an end for employees, a breach of trust has grown between workers and their bosses. After all, would you trust your leaders if there was no reciprocal benefit for increasing *your* productivity; if you had lived through waves of layoffs, outsourcing, and offshoring of your responsibilities; if you had witnessed corporate misbehavior above you; and if you had an employer who was insensitive to your whole-life needs? This life-work paradox is causing employee disengagement:

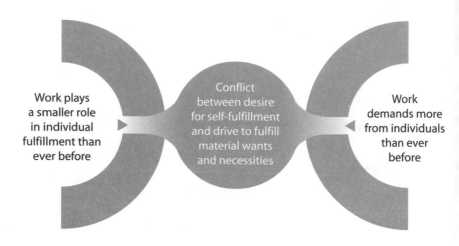

| Work plays a smaller role in individual fulfillment than ever before | Conflict between desire for self-fulfillment and drive to fulfill material wants and necessities | Work demands more from individuals than ever before |

Employees increasingly feel trapped. They need their jobs to meet material wants and necessities, yet work is demanding more from them than ever before and is less fulfilling than ever before.

The irony of this dissatisfaction is rich. As Brook Manville and Josiah Ober explained in the *Harvard Business Review,* "We live today in a knowledge economy. The core assets of the modern business enterprise lie not in buildings, machinery, and real estate, but in the intelligence, understanding, skills, and experience of employees. *Harnessing the capabilities and commitment of knowledge workers is . . . the central managerial challenge of our time.*"

The bottom line is that motivating people is paramount to a company's ability to survive, perhaps even more important now than it has ever been before. A new approach is urgently needed. This has moved the thinking on employee recognition from Expector managers—to achieve your goals you must reward, coerce, intimidate, or incent employees—to Altruist managers—people will meet any challenge when their achievements are acknowledged and they feel confident in their abilities. Recognition is still critical, but it's no longer just a path to get work done. It is a way to build our employees, teams, and organizations to a mutually better future. And that requires managers to help create what we call whole-life success.

Whole-Life Success

All those who work for you have a unique and complex set of values, personality traits, and attitudes that must be understood in order for you to effectively motivate them. For some employees, most of those motivators are work related. But psychologists have long known that employees who focus only on work, who find their only fulfillment in their jobs, and are motivated only by power, pay, and prestige are not as productive over the long term as those who also find fulfillment and encouragement in other areas of their life—family, fitness, hobbies, and education. Not only do increased work hours over a certain point actually decrease productivity, but overabsorption in one's job often leads to problematic physical and mental health issues. It also threatens marriages, families, and relationships, and can even weaken communities, as employees have less time to volunteer and mentor.

Effective managers create work-life success for their employees when personal goals are linked to work well-being.

Here's a plain but profound example. In one organization we visited, a leader supervised a security guard who had an outside passion for conservation. Most managers would have no idea how to blend this green interest with guarding a facility—helping this person be successful in both aspects of his life. This man's savvy manager found a way. He rewarded the guard with a new title: security and energy conservation officer. Now, during the man's security rounds, his auxiliary job is to turn off lights and ensure doors are closed to keep in heat or cold. This elementary change in duties and title has brought tremendous job satisfaction for the employee and a tidy cost savings for the organization. That kind of motivation is not possible without an understanding of the individuals in your charge.

Work-life success should not be confused with the old thinking of a balance between work and home. Work-life balance is a morale and a timing issue, ensuring that employees are able to flex their time to meet important day care demands, to get off early when their child is in a play, or even to take comp time when the ski slopes are calling. In today's world, work-life success means employees want to thrive in all their endeavors—whether making a nice dinner, running a marathon, or completing an important project on the job. Employees are recharged by stimulus from all aspects of their lives. They lead a layered life, with goals and fulfillment in all areas. In fact, it is a common need of all workers in all generational segments to have acknowledgment and support of life goals. Making progress toward one's goals, inside and outside work, produces satisfaction and engagement.

One forty-something manager in an advertising concern put this practice best when she said, "I've come to realize success doesn't come from being a powerful leader; it comes from leading powerful people." Indeed, she has learned to empower and engage her employees to achieve mutual success. To accomplish that, we must move from a rational perspective of management and take a more emotional view of leadership. This can be an intimidating concept for many leaders, but it doesn't have to be. While many managers fear that making an emotional connection with people will show weakness, nothing could be further from the truth. Today, the more we manage on the emotional side of the ledger, the more effective our leadership style is.

Let's examine the pros and cons of rational and emotional leadership. With rational-based management, a boss offers an employee a salary, safe work conditions, benefits, fair company policies, a good location, and a small share in the company's gain. Employees in a rational work environment realize they get material rewards for accomplishing the organization's goals.

However, employees also realize they are disposable resources for the company's productivity. Under this old model of leadership, it is certainly possible to build a solid work environment, but it is next to impossible to create a highly engaged, highly profitable work culture.

Why not? The old model has a glaring inherent flaw. Within this antiquated system, the relationship between employee and employer is transactional, competitive, and measured:

- Employees give to the company only when the company offers something in return (for example, in exchange for compensation, employees give to the company only the time and effort required by their contract—sometimes less but never more).

- When nothing more is offered by the company, nothing more is given by the employee (since the company is free to lay off an employee at any time, employees feel no loyalty and follow the highest bidder).

- If the employer takes anything away, the employee makes a corresponding reduction in contributions (for example, when an employee is charged for parking that once was free, he may feel justified in taking a longer lunch or spending more time sending personal e-mails).

With emotional-based management, a leader is aware of each employee's desire for self-realization. She understands that each employee seeks to accomplish goals inside and outside work time and to that end, tries to offer the right work assignments, skill development, increased responsibility, and advancement. Overall, the manager is interested in developing trust by assisting each person in the process of self-realization, and she ensures proof of accomplishment through recognition. The resulting shift in employee perception and behavior is dramatic. Within an emotional-based management structure, the areas between what is in the employee's best interest and what is in the company's best interest begin to merge. Rather than seeing the company as a separate—and competing—entity, the employee views it as a partner in her journey to a better and more fulfilling life.

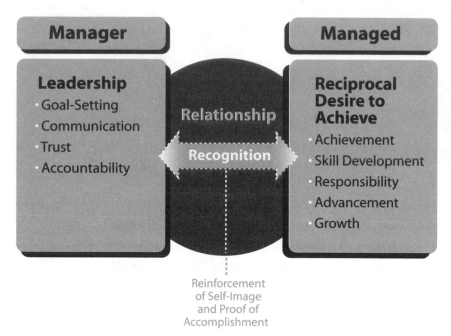

Where the old transactional model was mutually parasitic, with companies and employees taking turns feeding off each other's lifeblood, the new model is mutualistic, meaning that when one entity benefits, everyone benefits. Leading us to this finding:

Recognizing and developing the potential of individuals is the real path to leadership.

In our past, we would give a reward when we got a result, or we would dangle a carrot as an incentive to achieve a goal. Both approaches work—but for only so long. Instead, we must create an environment that celebrates accomplishment based on the unique individual needs of our employees, which moves recognition from the old model:

Commitment and Performance

Recognition

Business Results

To Recognition-Driven Leadership

Engagement of Individuals

Self-Actualization

Mutually Beneficial Success

One characteristic common to all the managers we spoke with was this: they want to be effective. They want to be the managers people are eager to work for. They strive to attract and develop talent. Indeed, just about everyone we spoke with—the Expectors, the Altruists, and the nonrecognizers alike—took a great deal of self-worth from their roles as managers.

However, we also discovered a universal self-deception: the vast majority of managers say they *are* effective. In reality, however, only a small percentage of the managers in The Jackson

Organization study are viewed as highly effective by their employees or by measurements of their customer satisfaction numbers and division profitability.

To reach the heights of effective management, your leadership style must become less focused on tangible outcomes and become more about recognizing the overall impact of your employees' contributions. This means you must get to know your people. You must learn to recognize them based on those personal profiles. And you must learn to engage your people in your shared success—building a culture of success.

It's time to take leadership to a higher plane. It's time to build a Carrot Culture. In the next part of the book, we'll show you how.

PART II

CARROT CULTURE

*How Great Organizations
Create World-Class Results*

5

Creating a Carrot Culture

We once had the opportunity to speak with Yang Yang, China's first Olympic Winter Games gold medalist. We asked this lightning-fast speed skater what she thought when that medal was placed around her neck at the 2002 Games. Her response was profound: "I was thinking, 'When I work hard, I can do anything.'"

When the employees in your organization feel that way—that they can do anything—you know you've created something special. You've built a Carrot Culture, a rare environment where employees are valued and appreciated for their contributions, which creates passion and performance among the workforce. As it did for Yang Yang, much of this passion revolves around the choice of the right award.

Rich Products Corp. in Buffalo, New York, understands the importance of awards. As evidence, take the example of Maria Grimaldi, a recipient of Rich's ultimate performance recognition: the Robert E. Rich Spirit of Innovation Award. As honors go, their firm's top award is a doozy. Grimaldi and her team of nine coworkers and their spouses were invited to take the corporate jet for a five-day vacation to a destination of their choice. "The prize is absolutely surreal," says Grimaldi. "But even without that, I've been surprised how much the recognition has meant to me."

After acting as the marketing lead for a team that moved a newly acquired company to a new location, integrated its processes and systems into Rich's, while increasing sales and making the change transparent to customers, Grimaldi and her team earned corporate kudos. Add to that the fact that they delivered the project early, under budget, and added millions to Rich's bottom line, and you understand why they were offered the corporate jet.

Now, says Grimaldi of the award she was nominated for by her peers, "I feel a need to live worthy of the recognition I've earned. I cannot sit at my desk and look at the memento of my recognition and not work that much harder to live up to the ideals and expectations associated with it. I feel driven to consistently display the kind of work ethic I am capable of, do the right thing, and go the extra mile."

Recognition Through Employee Eyes

What is it about recognition that inspires commitment like Grimaldi's? For the answer, look at the accelerator from an employee's point of view. Here is a supervisor taking time to do something personal and meaningful, something that she isn't required to do. It isn't in her job description. It takes away from all those important, secret meetings she needs to be in and all those pressing demands she has from corporate. Knowing this creates an instant connection on a different level. Recognition makes an employee feel that everything—every extra minute, every ounce of ingenuity and effort—was worth it. It can be an emotional experience they won't soon forget. They can see it. They can even smell it.

We've had an employee tell us that meaningful recognition for him was the crisp, faintly sweaty smell from a corporate booth at a National Hockey League game. For one employee, great recognition smelled like the sea breeze off the coast of Hawaii, an incredible trip made even better because the company picked up the tab *and* taxes. Obviously no company can afford that very often, so consider the busy employee who told us that the best recognition she ever received smelled like a freshly cut lawn that she didn't cut herself. Her boss had sent a yard crew over to her home. They even trimmed the trees.

One fellow who worked on an assembly line in Michigan explained that meaningful recognition to him looked like an engraved watch of a brand that he had always wanted (and now wears proudly on his wrist). A woman we met at a convention cracked us up by saying what recognition was to her: "The oil spot my car left in my manager's reserved parking space. As a reward, I parked there every day for a week. So there's an oil slick now under his Beemer. My usual parking spot is clear out in Zimbabwe," she joked.

Clearly, recognition can take many different forms. But whatever it is, the best reward is always personal and tailored to employee interests and lifestyle, given by a manager who cares enough to find out what motivates each individual. The funny thing is, managers who invest in choosing relevant awards suddenly find themselves becoming much more relevant as well.

Manager Relevance

Relevance means that you matter, that you have impact to those in your care. And in this day and age, nothing makes you more relevant than being the person who controls the carrot supply. The reason for this is rooted in economics: the shorter the supply of a popular item, the more valuable that item becomes.

With that in mind, remember that when we ask corporate leaders to estimate how many managers within their organizations actively recognize workers, they guess that 80 to 90 percent of the supervisors under their leadership provide little or no employee recognition. Indeed, that is confirmed by a Wichita State University poll that revealed just one in five workers believe a boss at work has ever publicly recognized them. And fewer than half of employees have received even one personal thank-you from their boss. That makes recognition a rare experience in the workplace. If you are one of the few leaders providing it, then you suddenly become extremely germane.

Says Perry Belcastro, vice president of operations for DHL's Gateways, "We can't have a wall between management and line employees. It will fracture our business. We want our managers to be engaged and to be relevant to the employee experience in a positive way. A manager shouldn't just be someone who monitors employee time or corrects them when they are in error, but someone who facilitates a positive environment for them, someone whom they see as an asset to their employee relationship at DHL, and someone who positively recognizes them for the good work they do."

Belcastro's got it right. It turns out that the most significant transformation within a Carrot Culture takes place not among employees but within the leaders who help to create it. The metamorphosis is simple but profound. The process of successfully creating a culture centered on recognition and the Basic Four teaches leaders that they have the ability to achieve future goals. When having experienced this ability to accelerate results using recognition, leaders are able to act with greater assurance in meeting future challenges.

Consider the transitional experience of a manager we interviewed who had been part of a team of programmers in a small start-up Silicon Valley organization. By his own admission, he spent his career as an average employee. He got average reviews. He put in an average number of hours. "I did the job simply because I could," he said. "I had the ability, and it paid the bills. But I didn't love it. And I wasn't out to win any races—probably because there weren't any races to be won at the company back then. They didn't acknowledge outstanding performance. They didn't have a budget to train me. There was nowhere to go as far as career development, so I was happy to sit still professionally."

Then a new CEO came on board and shook things up. "Boy, at first I thought we were in trouble. She was demanding, and I got a little annoyed and angry. She was rocking the boat. But then she called the group together and recognized me for my interpersonal skills—how I interacted with clients. You know, I'd always thought that that was one of my strengths. I mean, how many programmers do you know who like interacting with people? But no one had ever acknowledged that ability before. I think I had even started doubting myself and my abilities.

"As a reward, Jackie [the CEO] gave me a new project that I got to own. For me, it was like the starting gate opened and the gun went off.

"It's been like a night-and-day transition for me. I remember not so long after Jackie arrived, I asked my boss, the guy right over me back then, if I could learn about networking. It wasn't my area, but it was a place where our company was weak. I thought I could pitch in and also get a little professional development along the way. He wasn't appreciative. He said, 'You've never been interested in that before. Why the sudden enthusiasm?' I knew it was the feeling of being valued and the opportunity for growth and recognition that was egging me on."

When the fellow's direct supervisor left the company a few months later, he was finally ready to take his place as director of technology.

We asked this new director if, after what he has been through, he recognizes the value of building a Carrot Culture for his employees.

"Are you kidding?" he replied. "I'm the poster child for recognition."

We've often considered how much it would be worth to a leader personally to know that she has the ability to inspire workers to reach their full potential. What would it be like to have full confidence in your team's ability to achieve corporate and team goals? What does a leader feel when she's succeeded in creating a Carrot Culture? This Silicon Valley manager summed it all up for us in just four words: "Like a million bucks."

The following chapters are a guide to increasing your relevance and effectiveness using the Carrot Principle. We begin with a hard look at exactly where your organization is right now.

6

Are They Engaged
and Satisfied?

Before you can begin to create a Carrot Culture, you must take stock of how far you have to go to get there. You do this by measuring two basic factors: satisfaction and engagement. At first glance, you might not think there is much difference between the two. But, of course, there is.

A satisfied employee is happy with current pay, benefits, and atmosphere—so happy, in fact, that he may be reluctant to change the status quo through initiative or achievement.

Take the example of an employee at a trucking firm we visited. While there, we were interested to discover that one mechanic was paid as much as some of the organization's directors. It turned out that Russ had spent years before he joined the company tinkering with cutting-edge fuel-injection systems as a hobby—systems that now were used throughout the company's fleet. His current salary reflected that pioneering knowledge that he brought to the company ten years before.

But that was a decade ago. Surely other mechanics had caught up to him by this point. We wondered what Russ's contribution to the company was today.

We found him working in his bay at the end of a long row, featuring one of the few windows in the facility. During our discussion, he explained that he worked on just fuel-injection problems, which didn't occur as often as other maintenance issues. We noticed that his bay was empty that day. When Russ did get a job, he indicated that he took time with it and never felt rushed. And, he noted, he had become the shift table tennis champion. "Sounds like you have a pretty nice arrangement," we commented. He smiled.

When we asked Russ if, since he seemed to have a little time on his hands, he might also learn about new technologies, he shrugged. "I'm okay," he said, happy with things the way they were. And we had to admit that if we were in his shoes, change wouldn't be high on our lists either.

Russ could be the poster child for a satisfied employee. He is happy with his pay and position. There is no risk of turnover for him. He will stay forever, as long as he is not pushed to attain higher levels of achievement or work at his highest capacity. He is satisfied but not engaged.

The Jackson Organization's research shows engaged employees demonstrate the following virtuous qualities:

- Innovation and creativity

- Taking personal responsibility to make things happen

- Desiring to contribute to the success of the company and team

- Having an emotional bond to the organization and its mission and vision

Now, whether you run a team, an entire organization, or a single project, think about your own people-related goals and challenges. Then jot down the top five people issues that you face in your area of influence.

We asked this question recently of a senior leader in human resources at an equipment manufacturer. She gave us this list:

1. Developing leaders—our bench strength

2. Engaging our employees

3. Staffing agility—getting the right people in the right places as we expand globally

4. Retention of talent

5. Branding of our identity

A senior business leader of an engineering company in Virginia gave us these issues:

1. New opportunities/career pathing

2. Work/life balance

3. Conflict resolution

4. Recruiting and retention

5. Engagement

Notice any similarities? In discussions we've had around the world, three priorities appear on most management lists:

1. Engagement

2. Attracting and retaining talent

3. Building leaders

To boil it down even further, many leaders believe the most sought-after indicator of a successful culture is:

1. Engagement

After all, an engaged workforce is a company full of people who are willing to do whatever it takes to help the company succeed, including lead, innovate, and serve customers.

It's not hard to spot engaged employees. They give their all to achieve company goals. They are your above-and-beyond performers, your go-to people. We certainly want more like them. But they too have a dark side: they are the most sought-after people you have. With so many career options open to them, engaged employees are most likely to be the first out the door if they are unhappy with salary, management, or resources.

As we examine this dilemma closely, it becomes clear that neither employee satisfaction nor engagement alone can result in a Carrot Culture. A manager can't build an achieving workforce by solely focusing on engaging employees, because top performers who are dissatisfied never stay for long. Nor can a successful leader focus exclusively on making employees satisfied, because although they will happily stay forever, they lack motivation to innovate and perform.

The Jackson Organization's research illustrates the importance of each clearly. High employee satisfaction organizations report 20 percent higher customer service ratings than their low-satisfaction peers. They also report turnover some 50 percent lower. Similarly, high-employee-engagement firms report average customer satisfaction 20 percent higher than their low-engagement peers.

What managers need, then, are employees who are satisfied with pay, benefits, and the work environment *and* who are engaged to achieve.

What's Your Reputation?

Highly satisfied and engaged employees are as rare as they are valuable. In The Jackson Organization's survey of 200,000 employees, only 40 percent were identified as being both highly engaged and highly satisfied. That's reinforced by a 2006 survey of 14,000 workers showing 65 percent of employees are currently looking for other work. That's two-thirds of our people who are searching for greener pastures.

You can see the breakdown of employees from The Jackson Organization research in the following chart:

High Engagement Low Satisfaction — 14%

- Low morale and pessimistic about future of company
- Employees that are giving their all, but are not happy with their work environment
- High risk of turnover

High Engagement High Satisfaction — 40%

- Employees who are ambassadors for your organization
- Believe in goals and vision of organization
- Committed to personal and organizational success
- Low risk of turnover

Low Engagement Low Satisfaction — 26%

- Employees who are vocal in their critiques of the organization
- A distinct threat to your brand
- High risk of turnover
- Requires an exhaustive review of management and procedures

Low Engagement High Satisfaction — 20%

- Employees who are satisfied with their pay and position, but do not believe in goals and vision of organization
- Low risk of turnover
- Happy to "get by" and drain organizational resources

Take a moment to consider which group each of your team of people would fit into, or what percentage of your workforce would fall into each quadrant. It's a significant question because it's your workforce that typically differentiates your organization from the competition.

Says Allan Acton, senior vice president of The Jackson Organization, "In any service industry, for example, the perceived quality of a product is set by the behavior of the associate. Take car repair. I don't know the first thing about repairing an engine—my perception of quality comes from how I was treated, if the associates were kind and polite, if the shop calls me to check up on the repair. . . . These are the behaviors that will drive satisfaction and build a solid reputation for quality. But if even just one associate treats me poorly, the perception of quality is immediately damaged. Associate behavior, more than any other factor, is what will make or break a business. The data show it is essential to recognize and celebrate associate behavior that is consistent with the organization's core brand attributes. In doing this, associates will internalize those values."

Acton hits the nail right on the head. The greatest challenge for leaders in developing their firms is not introducing a revolutionary new strategy but engaging employees in executing their current strategy—no matter what it is.

Think of it this way. To your clients, your company is not your Madison Avenue advertising or even your dynamic CEO who's been on CNN twice this year. It is not your chairperson who's a real charmer at fancy-dress charity auctions, and it may not even be your cutting-edge products. In many cases, to those of us who are considered your consumers, your company goes no further than the employees you have on the front lines. It's the cashier who didn't smile, the vice president who talked too much on a sales call, the receptionist who smacked her gum during a client's visit, the bank teller who was distracted by marital problems and entered the wrong number, the equipment operator who held up traffic too long. In other words, your people are your brand, because employees either brand you as a good company or brand you as a company to be avoided at all costs (like the following national retailer).

When this company filed for bankruptcy several years ago, the official press release blamed competition from large discount retailers. But as we interviewed one former employee, it was evident that poor customer service played a part in the company's downfall. This young man explained that he had worked at one of the chain's stores. He remembers a rule that required employees to greet any customer who came within ten feet of them and ask the shopper if any assistance was needed.

"The other employees explained on my first day that the secret to survival was to make sure you never came within ten feet of any customer," said this young man. "They weren't joking. I saw employees turn around in midstride when they hit an aisle with a customer in it."

On the Internet, we found numerous complaints describing the "disappearing" employees at the retailer. One woman told of having to run down an aisle to catch up to an employee jogging in the opposite direction. She called out "excuse me" several times, without any response. The employee stopped moving away only when she said in a loud voice, "I can chase you down, but I'd rather not."

In that moment, for that customer, that "disappearing" employee defined the company. It also defined the organization for many of the people who read the Internet accounts. On average, clients who have a positive experience typically tell two to three people, while customers who have a negative experience tell as many as ten people. In this case, through the Web, this woman shared her experience with possibly thousands of other consumers.

The bottom line is that employees can build or pull down your market share. Engaged and satisfied employees trust your mission. They trust the service they are giving. They are ambassadors and advocates for your company. They produce results and can usually be trusted to create positive experiences for your customers.

But where do you begin to create an environment where employees are satisfied and engaged? Where St. Joseph Healthcare did, with research to determine where it was falling short. A few years ago, St. Joseph, based in Lexington, Kentucky, knew it had to make some changes. It was experiencing high turnover and low employee morale. It began with an organizational climate assessment from The Jackson Organization to determine the satisfaction and engagement levels of staff and find the best path for organizational change.

"We knew that we had to focus on the department level as well as the hospital level. We needed to bring everybody together for this to work," said Rick Tolson, vice president at St. Joseph.

Using the survey data to identify which components of the Carrot Principle they were lacking, St. Joseph leaders made organizational changes—and they didn't forget the accelerant as they added an enhanced focus on recognition. The result was dramatically more satisfied employees as indicated by a lower turnover rate.

Before the survey, St. Joseph was experiencing a turnover rate of 32.5 percent. Three years later, the numbers were down to 19.8 percent. "To quantify that, our reduced turnover brings us $3,680,000 in savings each year," said Tolson.

The good news doesn't stop there. In the two years following the initial survey, St. Joseph doubled its operating margin from 1.5 to 3.0 percent. It also found that as the organization improved, so did the number of employees willing to participate in the organizational climate assessment: from 38 percent to 77 percent in just two years. That is engagement.

How Do You Measure?

Workplace attitude surveys that measure for both satisfaction and engagement can yield important data. For example, The Jackson Organization's major research study reveals a statistical correlation between highly engaged employees and employees' positive responses to the following seven questions. We have listed them in order of significance.

Strongest Indicators of Employee Engagement

1. Employees in my department consistently put in extra effort beyond what is expected.

2. Employees in my department are highly motivated to contribute to the success of the organization.

3. Employees in my department consistently look for more efficient and effective ways of getting the job done.

4. Employees in my department have a strong sense of personal accomplishment from their work.

5. Employees in my department understand how their roles help the organization meet its goals.

6. Employees in my department always have a positive attitude when performing their duties at work.

7. My manager does a good job of recognizing employee contributions.

Here is a similar list of indicators, again in order of priority, this time for employee satisfaction:

Strongest Indicators of Employee Satisfaction

1. At work, I have the opportunity to do what I do best every day.

2. My performance is evaluated in a manner that makes me feel positive about working.

3. Conflicts are managed in a way that results in positive solutions.

4. My opinions seem to matter to my manager.

5. My manager shares all the information my coworkers and I need in order to feel part of the team.

6. I receive the information I need to do my job.

7. The organization has developed work/life policies that address my needs.

8. I trust my immediate manager.

9. During the past year, communication between leadership and employees has improved.

10. My manager does a good job of recognizing employee contributions.

11. I have recently received praise for my work.

Isn't it interesting to note how significantly the Basic Four and recognition come into play as indicators of employee engagement and satisfaction? Clear goals, open communication, trust, accountability, and recognition turn out to be the leadership traits that drive employee satisfaction *and* engagement. Interestingly, however, engaged employees demonstrated a greater need for goal setting and accountability than satisfied employees, and satisfied employees needed more communication and trust from managers.

Attitude surveys can be valuable in determining where your organization stacks up with the questions we've listed, but they can also be fraught with dangers. Knowing about these potential pitfalls—and avoiding them—is vital in reaching an accurate measure of employee engagement and satisfaction.

Conduct a Census Survey

Once you've decided to conduct an employee survey, the first decision you'll have to make is what type of survey to use: a census or a sample.

The difference is in the numbers. A census survey is sent to every employee, while a sample survey involves only a percentage of employees selected randomly from various departments. With a census, it is possible to gauge the opinion of every employee. Of course, it is also possible to achieve an accurate reading from a sample. As we find with consumer surveys of political races, very small sample sizes can have a high degree of reliability. However, to have the most impact, you will want results down to the department level, which is necessary to determine the effectiveness of individual managers. The reason for getting this up close and personal is clear: it's managers who are critical to the effectiveness of your organization and the engagement of your people.

"You've got to give every single employee an opportunity to participate in the research. For every employee survey we perform, this is one of the first recommendations we make to the client. A *census* survey creates the foundation for increased associate buy-in of initiatives based on the outcomes of the survey," said Allan Acton of The Jackson Organization. "Believe me, you'll need their buy-in when it comes time to implement those changes."

With proper promotion and employee-friendly methods of collecting data, high response rates are easily attainable. It's ideal to shoot for 70 percent or greater participation. That's because high response rates allow the data to be broken down into meaningful department reports, while maintaining employee confidentiality.

Maintain Confidentiality

Confidentiality is king in the workplace. The less faith employees have in a survey's confidentiality, the less they will participate. Of course, any research within the workplaces will be subject to employee suspicion, especially if morale is low. Many employees simply will not participate in a survey if they don't trust the confidentiality. A census survey is a mass survey and provides more anonymity to your workers. But you should also commit to not running data for any work department or area with fewer than ten employees, as managers may be able to extract individuals' scores and comments. It is appropriate, however, to share mean scores with these managers, just not specific data and responses.

Keep Response Rates High

If less than 50 percent of employees are responding to your survey, you can be sure that the people who are choosing not to respond have different characteristics from those who are responding. Think about a survey sent to you from a hotel you've recently stayed in. Chances are you'll throw the survey away unless you had a poor experience. That's what happens with low-response surveys in our workplaces. They are biased toward the negative, since the more dissatisfied employees disproportionately take the time to fill out the survey.

Take Benchmarks in Moderation

It's hard to have a discussion about measurement without someone bringing up external benchmarks. Ironically, they are the least important information you should consider in targeting improvement efforts. For example, many companies make the mistake of putting their money into fixing areas where they are below external benchmarks. As an extreme example, they might mistakenly spend money fixing parking issues since the score was so pitifully below national averages. But The Jackson Organization's research shows that an organization won't be able to raise morale by even one percentage point by improving the parking situation. Instead, focus your money on where you will get the most bang for your buck.

Let's say that your organization scored in the eightieth percentile nationally on the question, "I believe this is a great place to work." At first glance, you might not think you need to spend much money there since you are ahead of 80 percent of your peers. In fact, the reverse is true. Funds spent trying to get to the eighty-fifth percentile, the ninetieth, or ninety-ninth would be a much wiser use of corporate dollars—increasing overall employee engagement and satisfaction, which, as we've shown, has a much greater correlation to bottom-line success.

In addition, external benchmarks are limited because they only help you understand the current definition of "excellence." What if the best benchmarks so far are only average in reality, and your organization's employees can actually elevate their service delivery a few notches beyond the "best"? Then benchmarks would be limiting rather than motivating. For these reasons, external benchmarks should be used as just one tool among many.

"We advise [leaders] to look first to internal benchmarks and how they change over time," said Acton. "There is no organization out there just like you, so don't expect to get truly insightful benchmarking information from other organizations. Benchmarks to national standards may give you a general sense of where to go, but it takes internal benchmarking to get the detailed road map for how to get there."

In the cycle of the Carrot Principle, benchmarking is just one step in a continuous process of improvement. First comes research to determine where you are, followed by perfecting the Basic Four, then adding the recognition accelerant by celebrating your successes—and then beginning again with fresh research.

A perfect example of a recognition program designed to create real results surrounding employee engagement is found at DHL. With more than 400,000 employees, DHL is the largest express courier in the world but is number three in market share in the United States. Improving that position in the world's largest market has been a passion of many in the organization. Thanks to recognition, it is a passion now shared by an engaged workforce.

"What does it really mean to have people who are engaged?" asks Scott Northcutt, who is a member of the global leadership team for DHL. "We have shown that when you have engaged employees, you in turn have higher sales, higher customer satisfaction, higher productivity, and lower turnover."

Not long ago, after evaluating the status of his company, Northcutt and his peers realized that recognition would get his folks engaged and committed in their work. Like most other large firms, DHL had recognition programs, but they lacked direction and enthusiasm. "According to internal research, we discovered that we just weren't getting recognition out there. We decided we had to make recognition a key part of what we do—make it a clear strategy," he said.

Northcutt and Joan Kelly, vice president and now the Chief Carrot Officer, went to work to unify the workforce by reinforcing common values and beliefs among all employees. They knew their people needed to know where they fit in, what their purpose was, and how they contributed to the company. Most of all, DHL needed to make it clear to employees what the company was trying to achieve and what the DHL brand and "I'm On It" slogan stand for.

"If we could have all 50,000 of our people in the United States marching in the same direction, think of how much stronger we'd be when going up against [our competition]," Kelly said.

The answer for DHL was the Carrot Principle—creating a culture of engagement and recognition.

"We wanted the recognition culture to be infectious, for everybody to have it. It should be a great spirit that exists. We want every employee to feel that they own it and that they can be the difference between winning and losing," said Kelly.

And carrots quickly brought results. The program was rolled out with tools and training in the company's information technology (IT) department, headquartered in Scottsdale, Arizona. What's truly unique is that DHL's leadership not only trained IT managers on recognition concepts, but trained every single IT employee too. Every person was given a copy of one of our recognition books, was trained on recognition basics, and was tasked with acknowledging great behavior related to their goals.

In the first six months, turnover within the IT department decreased 27 percent as recognition began to have an effect on employee morale, engagement, and satisfaction.

Then the program began to be rolled out systemwide. Today, across DHL's U.S. workforce, Northcutt and Kelly say engagement scores are higher and employees are beginning to believe in the company's future and its mission. In meetings we've conducted with employees, it's obvious they come to work every day ready to advance that mission.

Northcutt adds, "What makes a company great is its heroes—the people whom other people in the company talk about. Everybody knows who some of the stars are, but does anybody know all of the stars? At DHL, we have an endless number of heroes we've yet to identify. We need to keep finding those heroes and getting them to believe in what they can achieve for us," summarized Northcutt. "That's what will drive our brand."

Carrot Principle managers build employee engagement and satisfaction by answering three of the most common questions—conscious or unconscious—employees have about their work environment:

- What's important around here?

- How can I make a difference?

- What's in it for me when I do make a difference?

While it may sound self-interested, that last question is paramount to the motivation of your team members. Very simply, people make decisions that lead to the most desirable outcomes for themselves. That's why Carrot Principle managers reward people for performing tasks that are valuable to the team or the organization *and* that help employees achieve their personal goals. Thus, recognition accelerates individual and company progress toward mutual success. That is why we call it an *accelerator*.

7

The Building Blocks
of a Carrot Culture

Recently one of our consulting colleagues pulled out his cell phone to make a call. The service bars were as flat as a Kansas wheat field. In disgust, he snapped the phone shut and mumbled, "I *can't* hear you now," making light of a popular advertising slogan (ironically for a competitor's service).

As this man found with his low-budget cell phone service, saying you are everywhere and actually being everywhere are very different things. Unfortunately, few companies manage to make the distinction. Instead of investing energy in developing the Basic Four skills and the recognition accelerator necessary to build a Carrot Culture that can follow through on performance goals, they often turn to the quick-fix approach that rarely works: introducing snappy new advertising campaigns or revised mission and value statements. Want to be perceived as worthy of trust? Include a line in your mission statement about integrity. Want to be known for great customer service? Take out an ad that says your employees are responsive. Want to work together as a team? Hang a poster on your wall about teamwork. If only fixes were that easy.

Recently Chester went to his local health clinic for help in fighting a lingering cold. As he lined up to hand in his insurance forms, he couldn't help but notice a colossal poster on the back wall with the new "values" of the organization. This particular health system had listed at least twenty values—twice as many values as Moses had (and most people don't remember *his* list). The poster touted a commitment to "respect for the individual," professed "intolerance for prejudice," promoted "their never-ending commitment to teamwork," and on and on. It was all very inspirational.

He also couldn't help noticing what was happening at the front of the line. A rather stern woman was seated behind the counter. With a perfunctory attitude, she greeted each patient by snapping the form they'd just filled out from the sick person's hand, scrutinizing it for a few moments, and then demanding proof of insurance.

Finally, it was Chester's privilege to address her. "That's quite a poster," he said, nodding toward the colorful values statement on the wall. "Do you believe any of it?"

The woman looked up, rolled her eyes, and kindly blew a raspberry.

Now, as a leader, you must understand that not everyone can be part of your exclusive team. As with this case, it was obvious this clinic hadn't hired the type of person they needed to live their extensive value list.

But the good news is that the vast majority of people you've got on staff will do just fine. Most can be nurtured to become more engaged and satisfied than they already are.

In our experience, hollow values statements, not employees, are the largest obstacle in creating a Carrot Culture. Empty value statements don't fool anyone: not employees, not customers, not even the executives who mastermind them. The reality is that corporate culture has to run deeper than the posters mounted on the walls. It can't be slapped together by your marketing firm or even by your well-intentioned leadership team, and then trickled down to your employees with the hope of execution.

In a Carrot Culture, managers understand this. They take and reinforce the organization's core values and define their brands internally by setting a clear vision and rewarding the right behaviors. As a great example of this, let's look again at DHL's "I'm On It!" culture. As we have spoken with employees and managers in this organization, it's clear that this is much more than a clever series of ads. It's how DHL is run.

That became abundantly clear when we heard the story of Leo Manley, a training facilitator at a DHL hub. At 10:30 on a Friday night, Leo received a call from a frantic customer. A specimen of blood was arriving in a package from France and had to move on to another location. The only problem was that the package had been held up in customs and needed to be re-iced, or the specimen would be lost. As a training facilitator, this clearly isn't in Leo's job description. And there was one really big problem to overcome: "We don't have any refrigeration facilities here at the hub," said Leo. "But I'd promised her. I said, 'I'm on it.' So I had about half an hour to find someplace to pick up dry ice."

Leo made calls to local beverage companies, but they couldn't help. "Then I figured ice cream, so I tried a local ice cream store. I would have to buy four pints of ice cream to get the dry ice, which I said would be absolutely no problem. The other issue was that they were closing in fifteen minutes. So I had to convince the manager to stay open a few extra minutes for me to get over there."

At the store, the manager provided Leo with the dry ice and the ice cream. Leo returned to the hub, re-iced the box, and then made sure it was on the next flight out. He also made sure the night shift got a bowl of ice cream on break.

Leo could have handed the problem off to someone else, but he didn't. That's the thing about DHL: it is building a culture that takes ownership of problems and sees them through.

Similarly, organizations that have developed a Carrot Culture employ recognition to reinforce a short list of company values and goals. If a company values speed and prompt customer service, it rewards employees who provide quick responses, knowledgeable care, and customer heroics. If a goal is accuracy, it rewards employees who perform with minimal margins of error. As a result, the culture becomes a rallying point for their people, who understand their organization's clear expectations, and for customers, whose expectations are met . . . and often exceeded.

The Value of Culture

If your firm were a computer, your corporate culture would be akin to the operating system, guiding how team members think, feel, and act on the job. If your organization were a living, breathing person, your culture would be your personality and very soul. It runs that deep. In fact, culture colors everything we do. Culture is how you do things: the rules, spoken or unspoken, that you play by. Culture is the foundation of everything you embrace, and the reason for everything you do.

For employees and managers alike, understanding the company culture helps us make tough decisions instinctively, without having to refer to policy manuals. In the best organizations, culture promotes collaboration and links diverse individuals throughout offices. Culture also can enhance respect between coworkers and clients. At the most basic level, it tells customers what to expect from us. Of course, culture also affects our ability as managers to attract better talent.

We've discovered that the more that organizations help individuals understand and fit in with the culture, the greater success the firm and its employees will experience. It's a bit like creating a giant mosaic, made up of thousands of individual pieces. In a corporation, something extraordinary happens when all the individual pieces combine to reflect the same company culture. The effect is absolutely awe inspiring.

It is not possible to achieve sustained, long-term success without a strong, positive corporate culture, which is what makes the culture clash that accompanies so many corporate mergers and acquisitions such a dilemma for leaders. In fact, the reason most mergers fail is culture clash and people issues, and yet, most senior leadership teams have little idea how to address this issue. In most cases during a merger, they either outsource the culture dilemma to consultants or ask human resources to figure it out while the rest of the senior leadership team focuses on perceived "important" pecuniary issues. Is it any wonder that more than two out of three mergers fail to deliver anticipated results?

DHL experienced challenges in blending cultures when it began acquiring various companies in the United States. Said Perry Belcastro, vice president of operations, "When you look at DHL over the years, we've had a reputation of going that extra mile for customers. That's always been our foundation. When we started to buy companies, we got a bit distracted at first from our core values. . . . Under the leadership of John Mullen [CEO of DHL Americas], we stepped back and said, 'What are the grassroots of DHL?' It's differentiating our brand through customer service. It's that courier going the extra step to satisfy a customer's needs."

DHL's Carrot Culture revolves around customer service. Others turn on innovation and research, while for still others, the crucial factors are zero defects and never-miss delivery.

At KPMG, building a culture that recognizes and rewards outstanding performance is always top of mind. Said Joe Maiorano, the executive director of human resources, "Whatever you read about supportive cultures says you need commitment from the top. We have commitment from our chairman and CEO to be a great place for all of our people to build a career and work. Recognition is a component of being an employer of choice, and leaders are accountable to recognize their individuals' and teams' performance."

We've found that great cultures are built best by frequent,

specific, and timely team recognition celebrations and individual recognition. They are places where the recognition doesn't just trickle along; it flows. At KPMG, for instance, 60 percent of employees received an award of value in a twelve-month period we examined, and many of those employees received multiple awards. In fact, with 19,000 eligible employees in the United States, the firm distributed 36,000 awards—90 percent of which were of the above-and-beyond variety. That means 11,400 KPMG employees received an award of value, and on average those great performers received three tangible awards during the year. That's a lot of recognition for those top achievers. But it's necessary for one big reason: great managers realize that their best performers are not only the most courted by outside firms, but are also often, ironically, the most insecure people in the organization.

That point bears repeating. In many cases, it's insecurity that drives many high achievers to perform so well and so consistently. Great cultures are sensitive to our needy natures, and they celebrate a lot—not only individual achievement but team successes too. For example, they celebrate corporate milestones: perhaps joining the New York Stock Exchange, opening the first office in Asia, reaching thirty years in business, forming a new alliance or partnership, introducing ecosensitive environmental standards, reaching a sales goal, launching a new product, and so on. Leaders in effective cultures realize events occur at least every year that are cause for commemoration, and they know that no organization can possibly celebrate too much.

"We often ask audiences if they think their companies celebrate success enough, and typically no more than 10 percent of the crowd says yes," said business gurus Jack and Suzy Welch. "What a lost opportunity. Celebrating victories along the way is an amazingly effective way to keep people engaged on the whole journey. And we're not talking about celebrating just the big wins."

What's most interesting is what happens to the psyche of

people in celebrating cultures. They start to believe that they are part of a company of champions, and that generates pride. Employees can't help but think, "We are always celebrating. So we must be winning." And that means that even when employees find themselves behind in a goal, they seem to band together to find a way to pull out a victory.

Authors Deal and Key explain the value of frequent celebrations within a corporate culture this way, "They bond people together and connect us to shared values. . . . When everything is going well, ritual occasions allow us to revel in our glory. When times are tough, ceremonies draw us together, kindling hope and faith that better times lie ahead."

Unfortunately, the inverse is true in organizations where excellence is expected, not rewarded, and tough times are dealt with harshly. Not only are these organizations no fun to work in, they fail to drive long-term outstanding results.

Building a culture that celebrates is a key responsibility of a leader. When celebrations stop, we've found achievement slows to a trickle.

The Building Blocks of Recognition

Great organizations and effective managers create a Carrot Culture one person at a time by using a variety of inclusive and meaningful recognition experiences. Fortunately, you don't have to reinvent the wheel every time you recognize. Here are four of the most common forms of recognition that make up the backbone of a healthy recognition culture:

- Day-to-day recognition: These are the pats on the back, the handwritten notes, the team lunches, on-the-spot award certificates, the gifts of thanks, and other ways you regularly praise and express gratitude to employees. This is often low-cost but always high-touch recognition.

- **Above-and-beyond recognition:** When your people go above and beyond, they deserve a more formal response from the organization. These awards provide a structured way to reward significant achievements that support the company's core values and business goals—whether the achievement of a sales goal, the implementation of an innovative idea, or providing exceptional customer service, for example.

- **Career recognition:** Most organizations provide a formal program to recognize people on the anniversary of their hiring date, giving managers a prime opportunity to highlight cumulative contributions. In most organizations, this is the most underused vehicle for rewarding and engaging employees.

- **Celebration events:** These celebrations reinforce your brand and thank everyone in a team, division, or an entire organization. Events to celebrate include the successful completion of a key project, achievement of record results, company anniversaries, or new product launches.

These four recognition types are the essential tools of a Carrot Culture, and it's vital to know how to use them. Ongoing training will help managers understand the *why* of recognition and learn the details of *how.*

Let's start by examining the basic recognition tools and how a blend of informal and formal recognition provides numerous opportunities for managers to recognize and engage their people.

Day-to-Day Recognition

It's called many things: informal, ongoing, ad hoc, or on-the-spot recognition. Three words to remember when providing this type of recognition are:

- Frequent
- Specific
- Timely

Make It Frequent

Day-to-day praise and recognition must be frequent. Gallup's research shows that for employees to feel valued and committed to a workplace, they need to receive some form of recognition every seven days. Counting just workdays, that's thirty-five times a year. However, that doesn't mean you'll be handing out Rolex watches every week. Instead, employees are interested in verbal reinforcement of their work. Managers who earn the most trust and dedication of their people do so with many simple yet powerful actions: writing a sincere note of thanks, sending a food basket to the home of an employee, highlighting a team member's performance in a staff meeting, doing their least favorite task for a day, sending an e-card of praise to an employee and copying your boss, and so on.

While this type of frequent praise may be a commonsense practice in our personal lives, it's a concept that isn't applied nearly enough in business. At work, managers too often act like the misanthropic husband who was criticized by his wife for never expressing affection. He replied, "Look, I told you I loved you when we were dating. If that ever changes, I'll let you know." That approach rarely works at home and rarely flies at work. In our personal lives, we tell the people we care about that they matter just about every day. We say we love them (or at least we should). The workplace equivalent of "I love you," is "Thanks." (Don't get those two mixed up, by the way.)

Ed Zobeck, vice president of the Auto Club Group, a 6,000-person organization with subsidiaries such as the AAA in Michigan, Wisconsin, Nebraska, and Minnesota, has become a believer in what he calls the "power of the thank-you." When we met Ed a few years ago, we left him with a very simple thank-you "checkbook" out of one of our manager's recognition tool kits. The checkbook holds thirty or so notes in the stack, and each says "thanks" and requires writing a specific note to the recipient.

Explains Ed, "I went back to my office and was reading through some really good work that one of our lawyers had done for me on a particularly vexing issue. I jotted out a quick thank-you check to him and dropped it in the interoffice mail. A couple of days later, one of my managers stepped into my office and said, 'You should have seen what you did.' I was appalled and asked, 'What did I do?' She said that the lawyer was in near tears when he got my note. He told her that he'd worked for the company for eight years, and this was the first time anyone ever thanked him."

Ed went on to add that the attorney's boss is a great person, as are his coworkers. "It's not that they're bad people, but culturally we had gotten away from the simple 'power of the thank-you' that is timely and specific. So I make it a point whenever I can to stop myself and stop whomever it is I want to thank, look them in the eye, and thank them very specifically for what they've done. Better yet, if they're with a group of people, I try to do it with others around. We call it a staff huddle—we'll pull together as many staff as are available."

Making day-to-day recognition part of your management style takes practice before it becomes natural. One way to remember is to keep a photocopy of the Recognition Frequency Log in your planner. Make a list of your direct reports, and for the next few weeks keep track of the number of times you recognize each of your people. Your goal is to establish a habit of weekly recognition for each person. (This and other forms are downloadable at carrots.com.)

RECOGNITION FREQUENCY LOG

My Team Members	Week 1	Week 2	Week 3	Week 4
EXAMPLE: Sue Smith	Extra Effort	Dealt with tough customer issue		Had great idea for team development

Try using the frequency log for just four weeks. Then take a few minutes to think about what you have learned about yourself, your team, and recognition as a leadership tool.

Be Specific

In addition to being frequent, recognition must be specific. Nonspecific praise is actually disheartening for an employee, since it implies that the manager has no idea of the unique value he or she brings to the team. Many managers who offer this type of general praise may think they are rewarding the entire team with comments such as, "Thanks, everyone, for all your hard work," or "You all make me proud." But such general praise has no effect and has even been shown to have a negative impact on those in your charge. It reminds us of this wonderful cartoon by James Stevenson we found in the *New Yorker* years ago.

"Keep up the good work, whatever it is, whoever you are."

Think about it this way. If the significant other you had a hopeless crush on in high school had gushed out loud, "I love all the guys [or girls] in my class. They're all so good looking and funny," would that have toasted our marshmallows? Of course not. As ego-driven creatures, we like to know what's unique about us.

A simple way we can start to express appreciation specifically is by writing a stack of thank-you notes at the end of every week, recalling what others have done to help us. Another is by

sending at least one specific e-mail daily outlining what someone has done that's great, or by providing a verbal pat on the
back once a day with specific praise. By doing so, we provide
gentle reminders to our people that they are important and that
what they are doing is valued.

Here are two simple examples of handwritten notes. One is
so general it will quickly find the trash can. The other, due to its
specificity, has the potential to be kept and valued.

> Chad,
>   Great work! You really are the best. I value all you do for us. You
> are just such a great asset. Keep up the good work.
>   Adrian

> Angie,
>   Thanks for your work in creating the new training workbook. You
> had to pull together creative people, got permission for the con-
> tent, worked well with the outside copy center folks, and were able
> to meet a very tough deadline—getting it to the client on time.
> Without those materials, and without the quality you brought to
> the project, there would have been no workshop. I can always
> count on you to take ownership and keep our clients top of mind.
> Thanks again!
>   Chester

What did we learn here other than that Chester is better at
writing thank-you notes? The first note is ineffective not because of its brevity, but because it shows a distinct lack of
knowledge of the employee and his value. Underline this: *General praise has no impact.*

One last note on specificity. Day-to-day recognition does not
have to relate to your core goals as a team or organization. This
type of praise and recognition may reward something as simple
as extra effort, a job well done, a smart idea, great service, or a
team success.

Make It Timely

Day-to-day recognition should be timely to the action. After all, that's the whole point of calling it "day-to-day." It's frustrating for people when they do something great and hear no praise. To be recognized days, weeks, or even a month later is of some reward, but in 99 percent of cases, a manager who puts it off will forget it. If we want to reinforce the right behaviors, we must reward them in a timely fashion.

If you need an illustration of this principle, try missing your spouse's birthday by a day. What's the reaction? In our experience, we've found it's difficult to get a good night's sleep on the couch. It's equally difficult to get the best effort out of an employee who feels overlooked. Timeliness communicates we are paying attention and that our team members are eminently valuable and necessary to our team's success.

In focus groups and manager interviews, we found many leaders reaping the rewards of giving frequent, specific, and timely day-to-day recognition. And yet as effective as these rewards can be, there are mythical landmines for some managers, which is why some leaders we spoke with chose not to recognize at all. They were paralyzed by fears of what to say, or what actions to recognize, or even what to give. Said one fellow in the nonrecognizing group, "My wife doesn't like the gifts I get her. Why would I try getting something for the people who work for me?"

The managers we met with who cared instinctively about their employees as individuals—the Altruists—took a few minutes more and found out what their employees valued. They had learned, very early in their employees' tenure, what potential rewards each person would value. Based on the information obtained from employee interviews and interactions, the Altruist managers strove to make award choices that were unique to the people in their charge. In other cases, their organizations had given them tools to allow employees to choose their own rewards.

The following chart can help you get to know your employees—their strengths and unique triggers. Some of the answers will come from direct questions you pose to your people. Others will come over time as you work with your folks and learn what matters most to each. The main point is this: the answers will be filled in as you consistently apply yourself to getting to know those in your charge.

Need	Name	Name	Name
Career Aspiration			
What is Most Important to this Person			
Strengths to Develop			
What Forms of Recognition and Awards Does This Person Most Value			
Recognition Ideas for...			

In the focus groups, we heard quite a few Expector managers—those who offer rewards with an expectation of some performance in return—who admitted that they rarely recognize individuals with day-to-day rewards. Instead, they focus almost all their ad hoc recognition efforts on teams. Why? First, it's easy. Managers are busy, and by only rewarding teams, they don't have to get to know their people individually. Second, it avoids confrontation. Expector managers are worried about jealousy arising if one person is recognized and another isn't. "So I just take my team out to lunch now and then," said one woman.

It's a nice idea. Too bad it doesn't work.

Now, certainly, great managers drive results by celebrating group successes with their teams: the achievement of a safety, sales, or performance goal; the completion of a big project; the collective improvement of a vital process. But they also take the time to get to know the people who work for them so they can offer individualized recognition. Again, we didn't say, "Get to know your 'employees.'" That's much too limiting. Effective recognition requires you to look beyond the workplace to your people's hobbies, families, likes, and dislikes. Get to know the whole person. And that requires you to get out of your office on a regular basis.

Many managers set a goal to get out and interact with their team for thirty minutes each day. They schedule it into their days just like a meeting. We suggest you take a small notebook along with you during these visits and pencil down some thoughts. Periodically, it pays to pull out this notebook and take a look at what you know about each employee. Evaluate which person you know the least well and set a goal to spend more time with that person.

Rather than inviting employees to your work space, where they might feel inhibited, we suggest you spend time with them in their work environments. You already know what is hanging on your office walls. But what is on their walls? What is on their desks? What books are they reading at lunch? What did they do over the weekend for fun?

As you get better acquainted with the people on your team, you're ready to provide "spontaneous" day-to-day recognition that is tailored to their individual interests and needs. To help you get started, Chapter 10 lists 125 of the best ideas we've heard—that's about two and half per week. And if you want

365 ideas, you can pick up a copy of our book *A Carrot a Day.* Some of the ideas listed will work for you. The others? Well, you'll wonder what we were thinking by wasting the ink. That's fine. Some ideas work in some cultures with some people, and others don't. Find the ones that fit the individuals in your department—or make up your own.

It might feel awkward at first to match day-to-day rewards with the individuals you manage, but keep at it. Whoever said you can't teach an old dog new tricks obviously never met a hungry dog. More presentation tips, training resources, and a monthly newsletter are available at carrots.com. We also recommend logging on to thanks.com for some great e-cards, recognition ideas, and recognition gifts.

After you've worked at it for awhile, you'll look back and realize how far you've come. We guarantee it will be exhilarating and energizing.

And just in time. Your next job is to retarget your formal awards. No- and low-cost recognition will take you only so far. For more important contributions related to your goals, to commemorate team or organizational accomplishments, or to celebrate a career achievement, a handwritten note won't do.

Above-and-Beyond Recognition

A 2005 global workforce study from Towers Perrin has found that 86 percent of the world's employees are not willing to go the extra mile for their employers. That's almost nine out of ten people who won't stay late, work harder, give you their best ideas, or go above-and-beyond for their bosses. They are the disgruntled majority.

Thank heavens, then, for the engaged minority. In our research into return on investment and recognition, we found not only that organizations and teams that are effective at recognizing excellence are substantially more profitable, but they have employees who are willing to go further, stay later, and take on more. And it's no wonder. Just imagine what would happen to your productivity if that 86 percent who won't go the extra mile became 50 percent or 25 percent.

In focusing on improving above-and-beyond awards, it's best to focus on three words: *value, impact,* and *personal.* The acronym for these three words is VIP, and together they make up three "very important principles." Here's what we mean.

First: Value

When you allow above-and-beyond awards to degrade into a popularity contest or give awards for nominal achievements like "being my favorite," or "trying really hard," you might as well abandon the attempt. These types of performance awards work only when they reward behaviors that support and further your corporate values. Awards should be presented for:

> Significant achievements: Great performances, excellent results, and actions that further your team or organization's core values
>
> Ideas: Generating a cost-saving or improvement idea that provides real financial benefit to your organization
>
> Sales: Achieving overall or area sales targets, winning new accounts, retaining your best customers, upgrading existing customers, selling a specific product, and so on

At KPMG for example, recognition is aimed at rewarding outstanding performance in relation to the firm's seven core values, which include working together as a team and leading by example. The values provide structure for awards, said Joe Maiorano, the executive director of human resources: "When individuals or teams demonstrate an ability to bring out the best from one another's talents, experiences, and cultures, with complex client situations under challenging deadlines, KPMG believes it's important to recognize this type of behavior. It's motivating for those who are rewarded and motivates their colleagues to perform at similar levels."

KPMG has confirmed in its culture what our study of recognition and bottom-line results discovered: in organizations where employees feel recognized for their contributions or "excellence," financials are significantly higher. Aligning this kind of performance award with your corporate values will help ensure that employees excel in those areas.

Second: Impact

The other day, a neighbor's five-year-old had acquired a grubby dollar bill that was half poking out of a front pocket. Spying a handful of pennies we had on the counter, he pulled out the disheveled bill and offered to make a trade straight across. To his young mind, this seemed like a great deal. After all, weren't there more coins than this silly piece of paper? The trade, however, would not have been equitable.

When giving a performance award, it is even more critical that the perceived value of the award equate to the impact of the achievement—at least symbolically. Let's say your phone system goes down and your customers can't place their orders. That's a big problem for any firm. Let's say experience has told you to expect a few hours of delay while your tech person methodically locates the problem, tests this assumption, and then places the fix. However, this time your tech support person responds instantly to your frantic call, finds the glitch, and has the phone system up again in a few minutes. You grab a certificate to his or her favorite Italian restaurant, and it is probably the right level of recognition for the impact this person had.

Now say a project manager has just completed an arduous year-long ISO registration process, working long hours and mastering difficult processes in achieving this important milestone for your firm. That Italian dinner isn't going to go over well (even if you throw in dessert). And yet too many organizations we speak with believe that movie ticket or dinner certificate recognition should be able to cover all eventualities. To have impact, an award should fairly represent the impact of the achievement. Assuming it does and assuming that during its presentation you link the impact of the person's accomplishment to the company value demonstrated, you are two-thirds of the way home. All you need to remember is the third component.

Third: Personal

A performance award is one of the rare times in an employee's life when everything should be about her, from the award to the ceremony itself. In creating a personal, meaningful recognition experience for the employee, your organization should also provide a way for the employee to choose an award that suits her needs. Barring that corporate involvement, it's up to a manager to find an award that will match the employee's interests, tastes, and sensibilities, which means managers must determine what will work best for each individual. You don't have to be perfect, but you should at least be good at it.

Next, the award presentation should be personal too. Choose someone to present the award who knows the employee well and works with her regularly. Her direct supervisor is usually the best option. Research shows that employees value input from their direct supervisors more than direction from anyone else. In most cases, the CEO or other senior leader is a poor choice for an award presentation. More times than we would like to remember, a CEO has innocently mispronounced the person's name or bungled the description of her accomplishment, turning what should have been a touching tribute into a sort of farce.

If you present the award yourself, take just a few minutes to prepare. Your formal recognition celebrations can do much more than simply thank employees for their contributions; they can focus everyone on the right goals.

A final word to the wise: an award ceremony is not a time

for criticism of any sort, even in jest. Phrases that start, "Let me tell you something funny that Amy didn't get right on this project . . ." or "Rob has come a long way considering where this all started . . ." never end well. Keeping the presentation positive and personalized to the employee will maximize the award's impact and power.

A GEM of a Case Study

All three VIP factors came together to create the Going the Extra Mile (GEM) above-and-beyond program at Rich Products Corp. in Buffalo, New York. As an industry pioneer in frozen food, Rich's has expanded its food products to become one of the biggest companies you've probably never heard of. As a privately owned, $2.5 billion enterprise, the company sells more than 2,300 products in eighty-five countries and employs more than 6,000 associates worldwide.

But even with a history of treating its people well, the company waited until 2005 to implement its first formal performance recognition program.

"We had a lot of informal recognition going on in various areas of the company," says Deb Gondek, GEM program co-creator and director of organizational effectiveness and communication for Rich's. "But several sources led us to the realization that we needed a more consistent, formal, and enterprise-wide recognition program. One of those indicators was our associate engagement survey. Feedback from the survey told us that recognition was something that we could improve on."

In some cases, the award value was not aligned with the impact of the achievement. "In the past, one department had implemented a program where it gave a $10 gift certificate to recognize extra effort and say thank you," says Shari Rife, manager of creative process and facilitation for Rich's. "It was very informal, without much criteria surrounding it. It caused real frustration with associates because an associate who cleaned out the supply cabinet was recognized in the same way as someone who implemented a huge project. Because they both got the same $10 gift card, it actually became a little demotivating."

So Rich's created a recognition strategy that would foster associate engagement and turn in solid business results. Says Gondek, "We put company priorities and goals at the center of the program and then decided on the best method for inspiring our people to focus on achievements that would most benefit the company."

The result was Rich's GEM Performance Recognition Program, a Web-based performance system that offers six levels of recognition ranging from a simple e-mail of thanks to a top-tier "Five-Carat" award that includes a nomination for the Robert E. Rich Spirit of Innovation award. Associates at any level can nominate another associate. And the program takes favoritism and subjectivity out of the equation by using an online tool that walks the nominator through a series of questions to determine the appropriate level of award.

Today, "Associates are paying more attention to what company priorities are and how they relate to what they are doing," said Tom Hauser, director of information systems.

Hauser is also one of Rich's thirty-two "Recognition Champions"—associates trained to act as recognition leaders and coaches for their areas. The champions provide ongoing recognition education and communication for each department and plant. "One of our most important roles is coaching nominators who submit vague nominations," he explained. "We don't just rubber-stamp a GEM award. It's important that we maintain a consistent quality in the nominations so that you don't devalue the impact of the program."

Hauser is eager to point out that recognition has made a difference for his team of technical experts. "Once people know that their job makes a difference, they say, 'What can I do better next time?' For our team, this means that managers and associates talk more. It means associates are recognized for outstanding work from users outside our department. It means my team—people who normally work behind the scenes—makes a better connection to the end product of their efforts."

Janice Horn, Rich's director of human resources sales and marketing, and co-creator of the GEM program, reiterated that focusing recognition on the company's core competencies is one of the reasons the program has been so successful. "It gives the program credibility. It's not just recognizing people who are favorites. It's people recognizing people for very specific things that have results attached to them," she said.

According to Maureen Hurley, executive vice president of the People Network at Rich's, "Before this program there was a good percentage of associates who didn't know what a competency was or didn't have any reason to think it applied to them. This recognition program gives us the opportunity to reinforce the importance and applicability of Rich's competencies and priorities at every level of the organization. It reinforces the kind of behavior you want to see people engage in day after day."

Adds Hurley, "Recognition will continue to be a major pillar for Rich's in our journey toward increased associate engagement. I firmly believe those places that have more engaged associates are going to be successful no matter what the marketplace does, what any competitor does, or whatever challenges occur. I believe you're going to end up with people who will go the extra mile every day. And that's what makes any company successful. I'm convinced the recognition piece tied into our whole engagement strategy is going to help us achieve all our goals going forward. Our COO, Bill Gisel, said it best when he commented, 'Everyone knew the recognition program was a good thing; we just didn't know how good it could be.'"

To create a recognition program that is as good as it can be, remember VIP. First, link recognition to your company and team goals. You'll want to reinforce what matters most—the *values* of the organization. Next, for greatest *impact,* present awards that match the level of the contribution and the interests of the employees being honored. Finally, make the presentation of awards *personal* and meaningful to the employees. In presenting an award, tell a specific, informed story about the accomplishment. An easy way to do this is to talk about the:

- Situation: The problem or opportunity

- Action: What was done, in specific terms

- Impact: The result of the action

- Link to company values: How the action contributed to the company

You may also want to invite coworkers to talk about the person's qualities and specific achievement before ending with a sincere thank-you.

One great thing about above-and-beyond recognition is that whether times are good in your company or results are not what you want, effective presentations will give you a chance to celebrate and reflect on the positive behaviors you need to improve your business.

Career Recognition

Decades ago, the only corporate recognition awards were retirement awards. Then early last century, businesses introduced awards to recognize career service. Today, these awards are used by more than 90 percent of midsize and large organizations in North America, and are increasingly used in Europe, the Pacific Rim, and other regions of the globe.

Why are these types of awards still so popular, considering increased workforce mobility and a move to focus on performance over tenure? Because career awards are the foundation of effective formal recognition. They build trust and establish a greater sense of connection with all employees. They validate employee efforts and thank people for the "thousand little things" they've done over the years that no one has ever acknowledged. They are a basic building block in creating a Carrot Culture.

Let's first challenge the way we look at these awards. When done right—within the right recognition strategy and with the right presentations—length-of-service programs are a perfect opportunity to recognize every employee on your team and, ultimately, the organization. They open communication channels and build relationships between managers and their teams. These awards also appeal to the basic human need to be included and respected.

When you think about it, what better way is there to build employee engagement and retention than to celebrate loyalty— especially considering that a recent Society for Human Resource Management poll found that three out of four U.S. workers are not loyal to their employers and are actively looking for a new job. Similar numbers were found by Salary.com, which polled 14,000 workers to discover that 65 percent were launching some sort of job search. And where do you think they are going? In many cases, they'll end up at one of your competitors.

We know loyalty is important, and we want to reward it. So why do so many of us do service awards poorly?

For the answer, think about the start date of your service awards. As you are no doubt aware, traditional programs routinely begin at five years of service and then occur every five years thereafter. We've even seen programs that start at ten years of service. But if you take a look at where most turnover occurs in your organization and in a person's career, it happens in the first three years. If you break down those years, most turnover happens during the first eighteen months. So how do you counteract that and reposition your service awards to build engagement?

That one good question deserves four others.

Author Quint Studer in his book *Hardwiring Excellence* provides four good engagement questions. We have begun using them in our work with organizations around the world and never cease to be amazed at the conversations they inspire. We recommend asking each new employee these questions at your first service award touch-point: after three months of service.

Let's say Laura has been with you for ninety days, and you've identified that she is a contributing, energized person you want to retain. You would say: "Laura, I want to speak with you about a few things concerning your first three months. To get a feel for how you are doing, I want to ask a few questions."

The first question to ask is: "You've been here three months now. Let me ask you, have we lived up to our promises to you? After all, when we recruited you, we told you that this would be a great place to work. We said you would do cool things, work with fascinating people on fun projects. Are we what we told you we would be?" Then listen. Ask more probing questions if necessary, but no rebuttals are allowed.

Next ask: "What do you think we do best here? I think *I* know what we do best, but you have a fresh perspective. I want to know what you think we do best." By this point, the conversation should really be rolling. These are great open-ended questions as long as you keep an open mind.

The third question is perhaps our favorite: "At your other jobs, I'm sure you saw things that worked really well. Is there anything you've seen elsewhere that we might be able to use here to make our company better?" Isn't that a great engagement question? You are asking the person to be actively involved in solving the problems of your company and making his or her work life better. You are showing how open you are to new ideas. And you are rewarding the person for the knowledge he or she brings to the job.

The fourth question is the clincher. "Have we done anything in the past ninety days that might cause you to leave us?" Right up front you are asking: Are you going to stay?

Here's one example of that question in action. We recently visited HSBC Bank Canada in Vancouver. After a lecture where we mentioned these questions, we received a note from Douglas Bottrill, a senior project manager. Bottrill explained that he had an employee who had applied for another job within HSBC.

Bottrill, however, was concerned that aspects of the new job would not fit the person's personality.

"After the session I went back to talk to him about his contribution to our team, and how if he were to go it would leave a big hole. I asked him if there was any aspect of his current job that he felt negative about. He admitted that he felt unable to contribute to the projects because of his lack of branch knowledge. I asked what would happen if I could have him work in a branch for a couple of weeks and job-shadow someone. Would that have an impact on his decision to leave us? He got this big smile and let me know he actually really liked working here and didn't want to leave."

Says Bottrill, "It seems like a double win. He gets the training and confidence to be a contributor in his eyes, and I get an employee who has more knowledge of our business and is happy to be a team member! Until I told him what his true worth to our team is and what he means to us, he was prepared to walk away."

What a great example of a manager using recognition to reinforce a person's worth, and then asking that fabulous fourth question.

We told you that thanks to Studer, great managers have used these questions for years, posing them to thousands of employees. When we have been invited to sit in with managers who are using these questions, at the end of the interviews we've often been able to ask employees perhaps the most revealing question of all: "Has any manager ever asked you these types of questions before?" In ten years, we have never met an employee yet who has responded in the positive. Is it any wonder employee engagement is so low?

Remember the words of Henry David Thoreau: "The highest compliment I was ever paid was when someone asked me my opinion and then attended to my answer." By the end of the three-month interview, you'll have asked the employee's opinion. Then it's time to attend to the answers.

How do you do this? Remember that survey that contrasted

what employees want with what managers think they want? In it, employees said they wanted to feel in on things and be appreciated. In other words, they want to be engaged. So once you've had this conversation and gleaned this valuable information about the employee, it's time to show appreciation with a simple welcome award presented in public, typically featuring your company's symbol or logo. You are limited only by your imagination. We've seen companies present a pin featuring the organization's name or logo that employees wear on their security pass lanyards. Others present an inexpensive watch with the company's logo on the dial. We've seen everything from company jackets to luggage presented as a welcome award. The memento is important, but only as long as the presentation is done well.

And yes, you must *present* an award. As you do so, say, "Every time you look at this welcome award, I hope you'll be reminded of the importance of the work you do and your growing role in making us a better company today than we were yesterday"—or something like that. The important thing is that you can't wait five years to show appreciation for loyalty in employees you wish to retain. You start at ninety days.

We also suggest you invite the employee to a follow-up meeting shortly after the presentation of the welcome award to discuss areas the person has identified for improvement. Prior to the meeting, review your notes and find ways the employee could be involved in improvement efforts. Then monitor the person's progress closely. If this assignment is handled correctly, it won't be long before you'll be able to give your first day-to-day reward or even your first above-and-beyond recognition.

We recommend incorporating the four questions from the ninety-day interview into your one-year service award as well, again along with a publicly presented award. Follow it up with a public award at three years, five years, and seven years. Starting at ten years, awards should be given at five-year intervals.

To use these awards to greatest effect, do not relegate them to a service award banquet at the end of the year. The year-end banquet can be effective as a follow-up formal event with partners invited, but only after employees have already been remembered on their service anniversary with a presentation at work by people they respect, surrounded by people they work with every day.

Here is a small excerpt from just such a service award presentation we were honored to witness. Bill, a silver-haired market researcher, was celebrating his one-year service anniversary with a manufacturing firm. He was surrounded by work friends and was smiling shyly. As he accepted the award, he acknowledged that in his thirty-year career, no company had ever given him an award in public. Here are two comments made during the award presentation by Bill's two twenty-something coworkers.

> Michelle: "I think of Bill as the department fireman. When we are all screaming 'fire' and running around, he helps us calm down and focus on one problem at a time."
>
> Alex: "He just seems to know what to do. As a mentor, I mean. He doesn't tell you what to do. He explains situations that he's faced before and let's you make up your own mind."

These are just two comments on Bill's leadership and experience from several dozen given during a ten-minute presentation. While the whole presentation took just a few moments of the company's time, those ten minutes made Bill's year much more worthwhile and gave him a springboard to launch into the next.

Retirement recognition is a standard at most enlightened organizations we work with. After all, how heartless would you have to be to send someone off into the sunset after ten, twenty, or thirty years with your firm with no party or memento? Today, most companies offer a selection of items that allow employees to choose a meaningful award—from traditional watches and rings to grandfather clocks and electronics. A beautiful retirement award can be the capstone of a career and something that will be treasured for years as a symbol of a career. So will the sentiments expressed in a retirement presentation. Although the recipient is leaving your employ, he or she will continue to be an ambassador for your company in the community.

Perhaps the most important people in a retirement presentation are the others who attend—those young and midcareer coworkers. For those employees, watching you pay tribute to a retiree is tremendously motivating.

You must make a big deal out of retirements if you want others in your team to stay with you through their careers or at least for a good, productive chunk of time.

Celebration Events

While most corporate events are forgotten even before the doughnuts and watery punch have disappeared, the impact of great celebration events can be just the beginning. Important moments in your company history can build employee commitment and loyalty, and focus employees toward the next accomplishment.

Whether it's your company's thirtieth anniversary, hitting a corporate revenue goal, a team achievement, or a holiday party, celebrations give you a hundred opportunities to thank everyone and communicate, "We're in this together."

Take the recent example of Intermountain Health Care, a 25,000-person organization headquartered in Salt Lake City. The leaders of this firm used their thirtieth anniversary as an opportunity to celebrate and honor employee contributions. Intermountain not only recognized all employees with an event gift on the anniversary date, it kept the party going all year long by including employee memories and historical facts in its weekly employee publication, producing large posters of company "wows" that were rotated weekly, and holding fun celebrations on or near the thirtieth of each month. As a large gift back to the community, the company sponsored an Emmy award–winning theater organization that toured state junior high schools with fitness messages. Employee focus groups helped ensure anniversary plans were on track with expectations.

As we spoke with organizers at Intermountain, they told us that choosing the right event gift was essential to the success of the anniversary. The item needed to fit their theme, "Ever Better," and reinforce the importance Intermountain places on its employees. Ultimately leaders selected a custom watch with the organization's logo and the anniversary theme on the face.

The watches were presented in April, when employees were asked to gather in groups around their system. The people were thanked in addresses by executives and then awarded the surprise watch. However, the gift was not given as in an "everyone-gets-one-so-here's-yours," type of presentation. The importance of organizational mission, vision, values, history, and quality was reinforced throughout the promotion of the celebration and at the actual event. The event gift acted as a symbolic reminder of the messages the company tries to reinforce every day.

In one presentation, Bill Nelson, their CEO, brought it all together when he said, "The gift is a symbol of what matters most—our time. I thank you for the gift of time you give our organization."

Nelson quipped that it wasn't easy to pick personal jewelry for 25,000 people. "But I hope that as you wear and refer to this watch, you'll remember how much we continue to value you. We look back on thirty years with pride, and we look forward, with you, to promise of the years ahead."

For Intermountain, it was a great year of celebration, capped with a touching presentation of a memorable award. And it left a lasting impact on the people who work there.

As people, we enjoy having our own time in the spotlight, but we also like to be associated with something bigger than ourselves. We like to know that collectively we are helping our team and organization move toward a brighter future. Event recognition is a critical piece in the big picture of effective recognition.

8

Carrotphobia:
Why We Don't Recognize

Despite the overwhelming evidence that recognition works, we meet leaders weekly with a bevy of excuses for why recognition won't work for them. Recognition isn't worth their valuable time, they tell us. Or it's too difficult to bother with. It's too expensive, we've been told. Or even that it's too frightening.

Here we list some of the most frequent myths of recognition we hear in training classes and those we have heard during focus groups and interviews. For the first few fears—the most common—we've included quotes from participants in interviews and responses to those objections by other managers. To the later objections, we provide our take based on our findings and experience.

Let's begin with *the* most common phobia to recognition, a worry we heard in every focus group we held in every city: the green-eyed monster.

"I'm afraid of jealousy if I recognize."

Said one production manager in a training session we held: "I've got seven people on my team. If I recognize one, I'm going to have the other six ticked off at me because they did the same thing last week and I missed it." The words were barely out of his mouth in that group when several people pounced on his insecurity. Said one: "Every week my VP recognizes at least one person. It's fair because it's happening a lot. If you don't get recognized this week, you will in a week or two." Said another: "You don't have jealousy if you create an opportunity for everyone to be recognized. We have two groups under me. One works with customers and gets lots of praise from the clients and sales reps; the other group just doesn't. Some of my peers told me not to recognize anyone because some of my people can't get those great letters from customers. I said, 'No, that's too easy.'"

Indeed, the two managers who responded were dead on. As we have visited teams where recognition is frequent and is aligned with core values to avoid favoritism, employees do not complain of jealousy. On the contrary, employees get more upset when recognition is rare and they are ignored.

Another angle on this is from leadership experts Jack and Suzy Welch who add, "Inevitably someone expresses concern about the people not being recognized: They might be hurt or de-motivated. This nonsense indulges the wrong crowd! If you have the right people—competitive, upbeat team players—public recognition only raises the bar for everyone."

"It's too easy to be inconsistent."

"It's hard to observe everything," one manager told us in a focus group. "It's easy to be inconsistent. I just know my dip-wad VP misses most of the stuff I do, or thinks it's part of my job. I don't want to be blamed for missing, so I don't do a lot."

While some other managers laughed at the "dipwad" comment, one leader in particular wasn't buying that theory. This Altruist manager explained that she recognizes her people when *she* sees something great but then added: "We use peer-to-peer recognition because it picks up a lot of things I don't see. We're lucky because we have a lot of things to celebrate. We celebrate the week's accomplishments in every staff meeting for fifteen or twenty minutes."

Said a second manager: "I keep a journal of who I recognize. In a healthy culture, you celebrate. You have a lot of successes."

Added a man who was almost rising out of his seat to be heard: "We've chosen people who don't get recognition a lot and we've given them an opportunity to rise to a challenge. And then we recognize them."

"If I recognize too much, it will lose meaning."

"I don't know how much recognition is too much, but I worry that if I do more, they'll just come to expect it or that it won't mean as much," explained one manager. In response, others told him: "I don't think you can thank people too much. It's like my kids. You can't tell them you appreciate them too much."

In a one-on-one interview, a man gave us an interesting sports analogy. He explained, "At a football game, do they hold applause 'til the end? Or when a running back gets a touchdown, do you say, 'He's supposed to score?' In our jobs, we expect [our people] to go above and beyond. But in sports, there's a reason the home team usually wins. It's because somebody is cheering for them."

Isn't that great? This manager, probably still in the glow of the recent Super Bowl, had really thought this through. To continue his analogy, there's also a reason that all sports teams award their trophies right after the championship game, when the sweat is still streaming down the athletes' faces: it means more right after the event.

Recognition never loses meaning, and it's best when it's fresh.

"I don't know what to give for what achievement."

Remember that manager from San Francisco who told us: "My wife doesn't like the gifts I get her. Why would I try getting something for the people who work for me?" It turns out he's not alone. Many managers are afraid of trying to guess what their people would like or trying to weigh what achievement deserves movie tickets and what deserves a bigger award.

We could spend a whole chapter addressing this concern—and we did. Check out Chapter 9, "The Carrot Calculator," for solutions to this specific need.

"We catch up with them at raise time."

Ah, the old standby of the lazy manager: "We'll remember at year end." The promise sounds good when you make it, but a few problems usually arise. First, financial limitations may mean you can't make good on your fiduciary promise. The old refrain, "We were so close this year," just doesn't cut it. And second, if you do wait, there's little chance you'll reinforce the positive behavior you want the employee to repeat and a much greater chance you'll simply forget.

Understand that compensation and recognition are not synonymous. Bonuses and raises are very important. They not only help us live the lifestyle we want, but enable us to keep score with our peers. But everyone, even upper-echelon salespeople and Wall Street high-rollers, care about more than money. Very few people will stay on a lousy job just for a paycheck. We need to feel that we matter. That's where recognition comes into play—helping meet those needs with specific, personal appreciation and frequent celebrations.

"Why would I recognize them? Aren't they just doing their jobs?"

Recognition gives employees the extra push they need to do their jobs just a little bit better. Beverly Gomez, general manager of the Friendly's Ice Cream restaurant in Hershey, Pennsylvania, told us about a dishwasher in her restaurant who was new and a little slower than other dishwashers. Many managers wouldn't reward an "underachiever," fearing what other employees would think. And most managers wouldn't dream of recognizing an employee for simply doing her job. Gomez is not like most other managers, which is why her restaurant has great financials and turnover that's among the lowest in Friendly's system.

Said Gomez of her dawdling dishwasher, "Recently she did something spectacular for her—got the dish area cleaned up in half an hour, where sometimes it might take her forty-five minutes. I gave her an ice cream cake to take home and in a one-on-one presentation I was specific about what she did that was great. Well, you might have thought I'd given her the world." And the reaction from the employee? "She's more open to me. She talks to me more often. Being a general manager intimidates a lot of people. So by my rewarding her with a cake, it made her feel more comfortable around me. Today we are much closer. In fact, when dishes start to stack, I dig in and help her."

As you can see, great managers reward frequently, and they don't hesitate to reward people who seem to be "just doing their jobs." The result? Engaged employees, better financials, and cleaner dishes.

"They want only cash as a reward."

The confusion may be rooted in semantics. Ask employees what they "want," and they most often will say "cash." But ask them what they "need" from managers, and the answer in study after study is "recognition." Remember that money is one of the least effective drivers of long-term performance.

While managers must pay market rates to keep the best people, "American business is fast discovering that monetary rewards are not only very costly, they are extremely limited in their ability to motivate employees," says Wayne Slough of the Center for Organizational Effectiveness at J. Sergeant Reynolds Community College. "No matter how much money a company might give, employees will soon become 'habituated' to it, and a phenomenon that researchers have termed 'reward inflation' occurs. . . . Failing to meet employee expectations could get an employer eaten alive."

There are other problems with cash. When people are striving for money, they will often take shortcuts to maximize their financial gain, even if it means sacrificing quality or integrity. Trust us. It's much easier to let them eat carrots.

"My tax department says we need to report the cost of an award on the employee's W-2 and then withhold taxes."

Some balk at recognition because of the tax bogeyman. It's a simple fix: if the award is of a high enough value to warrant taxing, then gross up the employee's wages to cover the additional amount. Under no circumstances should you require your people to pay taxes on awards you've given them. Keep this additional amount in mind as you budget for recognition, but don't let it stop you from rewarding great behavior. Trust us: the benefits far outweigh the slight bump in costs.

"When I recognize above-and-beyond behavior, it's most often outside their job scope. I'm more interested in driving performance within their job scope."

Many of any manager's people are what we call "Steady Eddies." They are middle-of-the-road performers and absolutely necessary to the organization's success. With that in mind, the bulk of your recognition with the bulk of your employees will be in the day-to-day realm—no cost or low cost—and you are going to be liberal with that recognition to improve performance within the job scope.

Also don't dismiss the fact that much above-and-beyond recognition is certainly what we call "in-role"—rewarding employees who behave in an exemplary way within the realm of their daily jobs. By their actions, these people set an example for other workers, build strong connections with your customers, and are the living embodiment of your core values. Fail to recognize above-and-beyond behaviors within the job scope, and you fail to drive continued great performances.

"She already gets too much recognition."

There are people in your organization who do receive more recognition than others—perhaps because of the high-profile nature of their jobs or their high-performance achievements. We've heard managers say, "The reason we don't recognize her more is she already gets a lot of recognition." Wrong. In our book, high performers are recognition sponges. Don't stop praising and rewarding, or they just might stop doing what it is you value.

"Employees say they'd be embarrassed if I recognized them."

Some employees say they hate the spotlight. Similarly, most people say they hate having their pictures taken. And yet when the snapshots come out, those folks look for themselves in the images. Of course, it's not our intention to have you embarrass shy employees. But realize that the vast majority of people will hold up just fine to a tasteful public recognition award presentation if it's brief and heartfelt, and they see others being similarly recognized. Keep it short. Don't make it a roast. Stick to the facts. Invite just the people they are comfortable with. And just about everyone will be glad you did it.

As for the truly chronically bashful—typically less than 10

percent of your workforce? In those rare cases, keep your praise and recognition private, but keep it coming.

"I don't know how much of my budget to allocate to recognition."

A realistic approach to tangible recognition is this. Most companies we work with budget about 2 percent of payroll, or about $1,000 per employee per year, for day-to-day recognition, team event gifts, above-and-beyond rewards, and service awards. Occasionally we've seen that number stretch higher than several thousand dollars per employee per year. But to start moving the needle on performance, $1,000 per employee is a good number. (Look for the recognition cost breakout per employee in Chapter 9.)

"We've tried this before. We had a recognition program that started well, but it lost momentum."

There are a lot of reasons that recognition programs either don't work from day one or seem to launch with gusto and then lose momentum. The most common problem is complexity. In our experience, organizations create overly complex recognition programs. They fear being taken advantage of by employees, so they put in multiple layers of approval and nomination. The irony is that while their defensive approach protects them financially, it also prevents the company from taking advantage of their employees' strengths and abilities. To rekindle excitement in recognition, start with a simple program that features day-to-day recognition, above-and-beyond recognition, service and retirement awards, and event gifts. Make sure your program is:

- **Strategic:** Aligned with your core values and goals
- **Simple:** Easy to use and understand

- **Measured:** Providing a return on your investment
- **Owned:** By your managers and senior leaders

Then when you relaunch, realize that manager training and ongoing communication are keys to success. Teach your managers why recognition is vital and how to use the program. Then keep excitement going with frequent communication from headquarters reminding managers and employees to recognize.

Most important, be patient and persistent. Realize that it may take some time for managers to believe this is not just another flavor of the month from corporate but is a real business principle that will drive great results and help their people achieve all they can.

"I don't want to recognize someone in one area of their performance when they aren't living up to expectations in other areas."

Yes you do. Otherwise you have no credibility when you coach improvement in weaker areas. Employees grumble, "He's always complaining. He never notices what I do right." Be bold enough to recognize what's good, and reinforce those behaviors while continuing to help develop employees in areas where they need it.

Remember, however, that it's important to keep praise and coaching separate. Take time to thank and recognize, but don't fall into the trap of praising in one sentence, and then reminding of needed improvements in the next. They'll only remember the "but."

"I tried handing out movie tickets for recognition, but my employees got sick of them."

If you found yourself stuck in a movie ticket or coffee certificate rut, then it's time to discover what your employees do value. A perfect time is during orientation for a new employee. Sit down with your new people to discuss their likes and dislikes. If you missed that opportunity, catch up now. Ask your employees to describe a perfect day outside work, making notes of the hobbies and interests they enjoy. Then ask them directly what type of rewards they would appreciate: dinner certificates, event tickets, time off, books, or MP3s. And try some of the creative things we suggest in our 125 ideas in Chapter 10.

Like all good recognition, getting to know what motivates your people takes a bit of detective work and a sensitivity that your employees may be coming from very different backgrounds from you. Age, gender, cultural background, outside interests, and other factors will influence their recognition needs.

"I don't have time to recognize."

We all are busy. But recognition should not take an inordinate amount of your time. The Altruist managers we spoke with took time out to recognize employees because it leads to higher productivity and better workplaces, and, as corny as it sounds, it really *is* the right thing to do for their people. They also relied on their employees to recognize each other, creating a culture of peer-to-peer praise. To quantify this, the effective managers we met in our research were not spending more than an hour or two a week on recognition. That's less than 5 percent of their time, but it was time that was paying off in big ways.

"Professionals don't need recognition. If I need to recognize my employees, then I hired the wrong people."

A few misguided managers believe that 100 percent of motivation should be internally driven and that recognition is used only to motivate weaker performers. There are dangerous half-truths in this mind-set. First, a lot of motivation *is* intrinsic. Employees have to want to deliver and excel, and it's certainly best to hire those people. But the hard truth is this: if you fail to recognize employee accomplishments, why would they stay with you to perform their duties? Why not go to the highest bidder?

Realize that every employee needs to feel a manager is watching and acknowledging her unique contributions. Fail to provide that extrinsic proof of accomplishment, and you fail to produce loyalty and continued dedication.

"I'm good at recognition already."

We often do an experiment at the start of our first day of training within an organization. We ask managers, "Are you effective at offering recognition to your employees?" On a scale of 1 to 10, most rate themselves somewhere between 7 and 9. Then we ask, "Where would you rate other managers in your organization?" Typically the ratings are between 1 and 3.

Isn't it strange? Here you are, in a company-mandated training on recognition, but you think you are in the seventieth to ninetieth percentile of effectiveness for this skill. Yet you view everyone else in your organization at the bottom of the barrel. Could it be you might not be as effective as you think?

Interestingly, the discussion then typically turns to frequency of recognition. Again, many managers think they are handing out enough praise and recognition and fear giving more since "it will lose meaning" or "they'll come to expect it." But inevitably, when we ask the managers to rank their peer managers on frequency, they put them near the bottom of the scale and say *they* should offer more.

Our goal with training is the same goal we have with this book: to help managers understand there are right and wrong ways to recognize and that all of us must enhance our frequency and quality of recognition. After all, have you ever worked at a place where you were thanked too much?

"I don't want to play favorites."

Similar to the jealousy concern, some managers are worried about creating "teacher's pets." That's why so many decide instead to "recognize everyone" as a group. These managers not only end up alienating the stars who make a difference, but reinforcing the behavior of their average and poor performers. When you start recognizing individual performance frequently, you'll be amazed at how easy it is and how nobody feels left out. In most cases, you'll also notice your employees recognizing each other and vying for more of your recognition.

"I don't want them to lose respect for me."

The managers who think this way typically aren't that worried about losing respect. They are afraid of losing the sense of fear they can instill—that they can fire, discipline, or yell on a moment's notice. These leaders actually worry that if they are too supportive, too warm and fuzzy, it'll be hard to get results when needed because employees will cease to tremble around them and obey them. Our response: You're kidding, right? Do you think your people will really work harder for someone who is aloof, intimidating, or outright frightening? Of course not. People work best for managers who care about them and root for them to succeed.

"They'll be suspicious of my motives."

Some leaders who have tried to recognize complain that one or two of their people think they are insincere when they offer praise or rewards. Often we find that the way recognition is handled is a large part of the problem. We even heard about an "ungrateful" employee publicly praising herself before the bosses could and then being suspicious of her manager's later praise. When the manager made recognition events more timely and added specific praise with stories, the problem remarkably evaporated. In fact, there are ways to correct most recognition difficulties with the general ideas we give in this book. Still, we admit that there is a small percentage of the human race that refuses to be satisfied, no matter how sunny their boss may be treating them. As harsh as it sounds, at some point you must determine if these people are harming your efforts as a manager and if they really fit in your team's culture.

"They'll ask for more money."

Actually, just the opposite is true. Employees who are engaged and appreciated are less likely to keep asking for more money. Who always wants more? Your whiners.

"They'll expect more recognition."

Yes, they will. Employees eat up carrots. When recognition is provided regularly, people will stick around for seconds and thirds, all the while turning out increasingly better results. And this is a problem?

After all these objections, the great leaders we met with in focus groups, to a one, chose to rise above their collective phobias and learned to build a recognition culture. Some acknowledged that it wasn't always easy; others admitted they had made mistakes. But like Charles Goodyear, they persisted, and they saw results.

Said one senior manager, "Employees who feel valued and appreciated are much more likely to be fully engaged and to actively contribute to the success of the business." He added that while compensation awards tend to focus on results, recognition is used to spotlight employees who should be viewed as role models for others within the organization: "To be effective, individual recognition should be frequent, specific, timely, and public. If these are not in place, it diminishes the employee's perception of the recognition."

He couldn't have said it better if we had written the script for him ourselves. And the comment couldn't have come from a better source: a high-level leader of a large financial institution—a man driven to reach Wall Street's and his clients' expectations. He is a leader who also understands that recognition is the accelerator of outstanding performance in his organization.

The good news is that this man's take on management is gaining momentum around the world. Every day more organizations are realizing that their success is built manager by manager, by leaders who have the tools and knowledge to motivate and engage their workforces. Within your own organization, there can be a leader like that, someone who grasps the power of the Carrot Principle and is preparing to use it to unlock latent employee potential. That transformational leader can be *you*.

PART III

MANAGING BY CARROTS

You Can Get There from Here

9

The Carrot Calculator

Remember the childhood cartoons in which a crazed scientist would enter a string of computations into a computer, pull a lever or two, and out would pop a simple slip of paper containing the answer to the riddle? We've often thought, "If only recognition was that easy. If only there were a simple calculator that could accept an employee's name, her interests and goals, the achievement, and how it helped advance the organization's values and goals, and out would pop a custom-fit recognition solution that was guaranteed to resonate with the person."

As a manager, *you* are the Carrot Calculator. But before you dismay, realize that this part of the book is designed to give you specific advice about how to provide those really motivating rewards to achieve the right impact. In Part II, we discussed the building blocks of a Carrot Culture. This last part of the book gets more granular, giving you tools to overcome many of the challenges of recognizing, including:

- Level: What level of award is appropriate for what behavior?

- Spending: How much you should budget for recognition?

- Awards: What creative rewards can you offer for excellent performance?

These tools will help make you more successful in using rewards to strengthen your work team, and will help your people achieve their full potential.

Let's get started by selecting the right level of reward.

Level

Sarah has just identified the bug that has been bringing down your server several times a month, and she has implemented the fix. She deserves recognition. But how much is it worth? A car wash, a thank-you note, a trip to Bora-Bora?

From our work with numerous organizations—from those with a few hundred employees to those with tens of thousands—here are a few rules of thumb for determining the level of an accomplishment.

Decide if the successful behavior is (1) a *small step* toward living your values; (2) a *one-time* above-and-beyond action, linked to your values, which makes you more successful; (3) an *ongoing* above-and-beyond demonstration of your values in action, which is making your organization more successful; or (4) an action, project, or behavior that has a significant impact on the *bottom line*. To know how to pick your carrots wisely, break them down into four types: thank-you, bronze, silver, and gold awards.

Thank-you recognition is for daily, ongoing encouragement of the small steps that lead us to success. After all, it's rarely the large things that differentiate us in our customers' minds from the competition; it's the little things employees do that make all the difference. Thank-you recognition is the most frequent type offered by effective managers. It is given to an employee who meets (but not necessarily exceeds) performance expectations. It is day-to-day encouragement for the person who is a consistent and steady performer, who always gets the report in on time, who is always courteous when making a delivery to a customer's home or business, who always has a positive attitude, who is the consummate team player, who gave an admirable try but didn't quite make it, and so on. Thankyou praise might be given publicly or privately by sending an e-card or a handwritten note, by giving something of *de minimis* value typically costing $50 or less, such as movie tickets, a gift basket, coffee and doughnuts, by using some of the 125 ideas we list in the next chapter, or in some cases, by rewarding with a more valuable gift if you deem the person's effort important enough.

Bronze awards recognize one-time above-and-beyond behaviors related to your core values, which might include an employee who cares for an angry customer and saves the day, takes on an additional duty, stays late to get out an important project, finds a way to improve a routine process, comes up with a creative solution to a problem, puts together a great pitch for a prospective client, finds the glitch in the server (like our fictional Sarah), and so on. Most bronze awards are tangible items in the $50 to $100 range. This could include the presentation of a personalized award, dinner for two, tickets to a ball game or symphony, a selection from a catalogue of merchandise, or anything else you can dream up.

Silver awards reward ongoing above-and-beyond behaviors. Employees are eligible for these awards if they consistently demonstrate your values by taking on challenging customer issues, work late weeks in a row, develop sophisticated changes to improve important processes, demonstrate outstanding leadership, improve the way you pitch prospective clients, mentor a new employee to productivity, provide exceptional customer care, and so on. If you know that at 5:05 P.M., after closing, Susan doesn't hesitate in opening the doors when a frantic customer shows up, she's worthy of a silver award. You do this with a tangible merchandise award, publicly presented, and typically valued from $100 to $500.

Gold awards recognize behaviors that produce bottom-line results. These may be one-time or ongoing achievements and are the highest level of above-and-beyond awards. These rewards recognize an employee who has clearly influenced your financial statement, perhaps by developing a new system that saves money, being granted a patent, winning an important industry award, breaking a performance record, landing a new account, introducing a new process to significantly improve efficiency, achieving a top sales goal, being part of a team that came together with the innovative pitch that won a big deal, or working from a customer service position to keep a big client in the fold. The level of award will depend on the impact. If the idea saves millions of dollars, then the sky is the limit when it comes to how much you will spend to recognize this person or team. These awards may include a cash component, but there is always a valuable tangible reminder of the achievement, typically worth $500 or more. Neglect to present an heirloom award, and the recognition may be reduced to a simple business transaction.

Take as an example an engineering employee we spoke with in a professional role in the Midwest. He had volunteered to put in double time to correct his organization's reporting software, which had been found to be inaccurate. "Our clients told us that if we didn't get it right, and right away, they would cancel their contracts with us. It was a deal-breaker," he said.

The engineer explained that before he started the project, his boss made it clear that there would be a big reward at the end. When the project was completed, this man waited to be recognized—and waited some more. Finally, he went to his boss's office and asked if he should really expect any reward.

"She said, 'Yes,' but the amount hadn't been approved by the board," he said. "She told me she'd let me know when it was approved. Finally, she came into my office one day and told me she had gotten a cash bonus approved. But instead of feeling excited, like I thought I would, I kind of felt like, 'Well, it's about time.' "

The engineer was told his bonus would likely be included in his next paycheck or the one after that. It did eventually appear—with no public presentation of a tangible reminder, no resulting feeling of achievement and pride, and no reinforcement of his above-and-beyond actions that other employees could learn from.

"My wife called to tell me that the bonus had shown up on my latest paycheck. She was the one who said, 'You deserved it.' "

The engineer actually turned out to be a better recognizer than his boss. Despite his disappointment, he went home and bought a card thanking his boss for the bonus and gave it to her the next day with a verbal expression of appreciation.

As this illustrates, even high achievers receiving a large cash bonus for an outstanding achievement need something tangible, and when it comes to gold awards, not just any award will do. You must get creative to match the award with a person's interests; the nice thing is that your spending will be justified by the return on the person's contribution.

It's interesting to note that many organizations choose a group of president's or chairman's award winners from their gold award winners. If you do offer such high-level recognition from your executive team, make sure you include at least several employees as recipients.

Spending

Remember that most organizations we work with budget 2 percent of payroll or about $1,000 per employee per year for day-to-day recognition, team event gifts, above-and-beyond, and service awards. Of course, that spending can vary, but we think $1,000 is a good basic starting point that will help move the needle on employee performance, engagement, and satisfaction.

Here's a breakout of anticipated annual spending per employee:

Day-to-Day (Thank-You Level)

- $0 annually. Every seven business days (or thirty-five times a year) you will thank with something free—a handwritten note, verbal praise, or an e-mail of thanks, for example.

- $100 to $200 annually. Four to six times a year on average, you will award with something of tangible but often de minimis value—a gift from a selection, movie tickets, a basket of food, or dinner or coffee certificates, for example.

Above-and-Beyond Awards (Bronze, Silver, and Gold Levels)

- $250 to $500 annually. On average at least every two years, an employee should receive a tangible performance award for above-and-beyond behavior. Of course, there are many outstanding employees in your organization who will receive several performance awards annually.

Event Recognition

- $100 annually. At least semiannually, you should be celebrating team victories with a gift, party, or outing.

Service Awards

- $200 annually. At ninety days, one year, three years, five years, seven years, ten years, and then every five years thereafter, it's important to recognize loyalty with a lasting award appropriate to their achievement.

This information is intended to be used flexibly, of course. Not every team or organization will fall into these general guidelines. Some managers might choose to put more money into areas such as above-and-beyond awards, encouraging excellence on a more frequent basis. Others might invest even more on day-to-day awards, encouraging their "B" players to hit their stride. Other managers who develop strong Carrot Cultures will invest many times more than this in each category. And those just getting started with a recognition program or looking to enhance their efforts will invest more in training to help managers understand the need for recognition and how to use the tools at their disposal.

A great way to track the frequency of the awards you present is by using the recognition frequency log.

Awards

With money to spend and an idea of the behaviors to recognize, it's time to begin handing out praise and recognition awards. To keep things fresh, you'll probably need some idea of what to give and a few good ways to remember to recognize. Fortunately, we've got a few ideas for you: 125 to be exact.

10

125 Recognition Ideas

As a rule, managers and reporters are a shrewd bunch. They challenge ideas, demand proof, and love to find flaws in any argument. One articulate magazine reporter observed, "There's a danger that an insensitive or naïve manager might try to recognize without understanding the key truth behind rewards—that each employee is unique, with their own motivation triggers, and the real skill of a manager is to find out what these are and tap into them."

We think this reporter has missed her calling; she'd make an excellent leader.

Perhaps the most difficult portion of the recognition process is choosing a form of recognition that taps an employee's motivation triggers. In our experience, we have found only two ways to do so successfully. First, you offer employees a choice of awards, which is usually done by your corporate group in establishing a formal reward program. Great managers fully use these formal resources offered by their organizations. The second way, for managers alone in their efforts, is in getting to know your people and what they value.

Becoming well acquainted with your people is certainly the road less traveled of management. But among the leaders we have observed who take the time and interest to personalize recognition, it has made all the difference in employee performance.

The 125 ideas that follow are just a short list of recognition starters. Many were gleaned from the managers we spoke with around the world. The ideas are not intended to be used in order, nor does a manager need to try even the majority—as no person could get through this full list without achieving sainthood. Knowing your employees, you'll be able to determine which will work for you and which will not. We would caution you to be considerate of cultural differences and other potential sensitivities. However, we would also caution you to not let fear stand in your way. As you'll see, there are as many ways to recognize as there are employees who deserve recognition.

To help illustrate how recognition can accelerate leadership abilities, we've grouped our ideas into five areas of the Carrot Principle: goal setting, communication, trust, accountability, and recognition. Most of the ideas in the sections fit the five areas. Some, however, are just fun reward ideas that we've dropped in at random places to keep things lively. You'll notice that most of the ideas are for creative rewards, but some are intended to help you get to know your employees—which is not only a necessary first step in offering personalized rewards, but is also a very effective form of recognition in and of itself.

We encourage you to keep an open mind with these ideas, and not to discount the entire list if you come across a few that won't work in your environment. With that said, we'd also ask you to try a few that might be out of your comfort zone. After all, a new approach and engaging employees in a fresh way will always be more successful than ignoring them. And who knows, the new way you recognize today may become the preferred method in the future.

Goal Setting

1. On a new employee's first day, set expectations high by planning a small celebration. Then send out an e-mail to employees about the new person and why she was chosen to join the team. Invite coworkers to stop by. Even better, present the new person with a card signed by everyone on the team, welcoming her aboard.

2. What makes your employees tick? Why not ask? Ask each employee to list the values that guide his or her daily decisions. During a private meeting, discuss how these lists compare with—and contrast to—the company mission and value statements.

3. Take exercise 2 a step further by encouraging employees to post their values list conspicuously at the office or on the job site. Set the example. Put a note on your bathroom mirror to see before you leave for work. Tape it inside your checkbook. Move the notes frequently so they are always unexpected. Remember that what is out of sight is often out of mind.

4. As a reward, bring in a fortune-teller to tell positive fortunes that relate to your core work goals.

5. The next time your employee scans the "What They're Doing Now" section of his or her college alumni publication, make sure he sees a familiar face . . . his own. Just because an employee doesn't blow his horn doesn't mean he wouldn't like you to make some noise.

6. Turn a responsibility into a reward. Ask an employee to help train a new employee in a job function where the employee excels. Explain in detail what qualifies the employee for this important assignment.

7. Tell employees frequently and sincerely: "I know you can do it." Victor Vroom's expectancy theory teaches that employees work toward goals that they (1) want and (2) believe they have a realistic chance of obtaining. If you don't believe your team can achieve a goal, it's almost certain they won't.

8. Invite an employee to take his spouse along on a business trip. Pay for the spouse's airplane ticket and extend the trip by one day for some sightseeing.

9. When employees have to work on a weekend, provide a catered lunch for them. Make it even better by inviting their families to join them for lunch.

10. Surprise your people by taking them to a blockbuster film matinee on opening day. Choose a flick that won't offend anyone, and, if possible, double the impact by choosing a movie that shows a team working together to achieve a difficult goal.

11. Variety is the spice of life. Give employees important tasks that stretch their abilities and are outside their job descriptions. Give them the training, resources, and contacts they require to succeed.

12. Recognition is a great vehicle to help achieve results and propel your people to greater things—but only if you remember, remember, remember. At the beginning of each day, put three coins in your right pocket. Transfer one to the left each time you reward an employee for a behavior that is critical to your goals, your customers, your employees, and your company. By the end of the day, the three coins should be in your left pocket.

13. Rather than criticizing an employee who is off track, make a positive "course correction." Define the problem in precise terms. Describe in detail what she must do to meet expectations. Then express your confidence in her ability to make necessary changes. Thank her for being part of the team.

14. Create a self-fulfilling prophecy. In the middle of a stressful team assignment, greet employees at the door in the morning with a hot cup of coffee for each. (Ever better, hire a barista to mix up designer coffees.) Tell them that you are glad to see them. Tell them that you are convinced their project is going to be wildly successful.

15. Once in a while, set a daily goal that supports your company goals. Set it high enough to make employees stretch. Post results on a big board. Host a quick award ceremony for the best performer of the hour. End the day with a celebratory dinner before quitting time.

16. The next time an employee on the night shift takes commitment to new heights, host an award ceremony under the night sky.

17. Nobody's perfect at everything. But most employees come pretty close in at least one area. Effective managers know this and make a point to find each employee's strength, tap it, and then recognize it. Set a goal today to identify what each employee in your department does best.

18. The next time an employee goes above and beyond for your organization, hire a concierge service for a week to lessen her burden outside the office.

19. Are people getting hot under the collar? Call in an ice cream truck to cool things down. When employees hear the music playing, invite them all to go get an ice cream on you. They won't be able to stop smiling.

20. When it comes to employee recognition, knowledge is power. Set a goal to find out one new thing about each employee today.

21. Reprint an employee's business cards featuring an exclusive achievement-level logo when he has achieved a certain goal. Make him part of an exclusive club.

22. Show you value employee expertise by creating an instruction manual featuring team members as the experts. Interview employees about their job functions. Compile your people's insights into a booklet that you can give to new employees on their first day.

23. Give your employees a spot quiz that will show if you are making the grade as a manager. Drop into their offices and ask them to go over the company mission statement and goals from memory. If they can't, reexamine your recognition efforts. Are you making the connection between recognition and organizational goals?

Communication

24. Take a lesson from the Boy Scouts: Be prepared. Carry gift cards to your people's favorite restaurants wherever you go. When you spot someone doing something in keeping with your company or team values, stop and recognize her on the spot with something she'll value.

25. Hire a celebrity impersonator to leave a congratulatory voice-mail message on an employee's phone. Choose a celebrity whom the employee idolizes. If possible, plan it so the message is received first thing in the morning.

26. Expand your vision by attending a conference on

recognition or reading a book on the subject (may we suggest one of our other books). Opening your mind to new ideas will make you a more effective leader.

27. At the end of each day, write down three things that went right. Getting in the habit of looking for the positives around you will pay dividends at the office, at home, and socially. It also gives you many things to recognize.

28. Make a commitment to call people by name and say good morning to them every day. It shows you see them as individuals, not just faces in a crowd.

29. Give an employee a gift card to use to personalize her office. When the office is redecorated, make a point to come and see it again. You might learn a lot more about the person.

30. You may be a great manager, but you can't be everywhere and see everything at once, so ask for help. Give your people a stack of thank-you cards, and ask them to recognize coworkers when they see them furthering company values.

31. To thank a team for a great year or achievement, invite them to your house for a meal or barbecue. It'll give you a chance to meet their families and will also let them meet your family. Inviting someone into your home is a big step, but it will build bonds of friendship and enhance open communication.

32. Personally deliver your employee's next paycheck to her. Before you hand it over, spend a few moments defining exactly what she contributes to the company. Trust us: it's never the money that makes a person feel like a million bucks. It's the praise.

33. Bring in a masseuse and a massage chair and provide

free massages. Employees will feel the benefits of recognition in their very shoulders, which carry such burdens for you.

34. Each day, spend ten minutes looking for someone doing something that furthers your company's goals. When you find it, recognize the person on the spot.

35. Make a list of what you know about each person in your care. What do they do at work? What do they hang on their office walls? Do they have kids? If so, what are their names, and how old are they? Then ask yourself: Which employee do I know the least about? Take time today to visit that person in her office and get to know her better.

36. On an employee's first day at the office, ask him to tell you about his favorite recognition moment from a former job. What did he do to earn the award? What was the award? How did he feel? Where is the award today? You'll not only get a good idea of what type of recognition he values, you'll also see his strengths right away.

37. The next time you are talking with one of your people, ask, "If you had a day off to spend as you wanted, what would you do?" Seeing an employee as a person outside the office is the first step toward choosing an appropriate form of recognition.

38. How do you recognize a poor performer? Carefully. The idea is to praise even the smallest movement toward valued behavior.

39. Anticipation can sweeten recognition. Before a formal award ceremony, visit with the employee personally and thank him for his contribution. Tell him about the upcoming ceremony, and let the anticipation grow.

40. Let one of your people open your eyes to something good she is doing to further company goals. Kick off a staff meeting by inviting each employee to share one achievement from the previous seven days.

41. Invite all your employees to recognition events. When employees see their peers being recognized, it makes them want the same recognition, spurring higher performance.

42. We have found that at best, fewer than half of managers even try to recognize their people. That means if you are recognizing, you have a strategic advantage over most of your peers and your competitors.

43. Take an employee who loves nature to the nursery and buy some plants or flowers for him.

Recognition

44. Don't send a card on an employee's birthday; deliver it to her in person. In advance of the visit, write on the card a short list of the person's achievements during the past year. Read it together. It will be one gift she won't soon forget.

45. Give an award that keeps on giving all year long: a subscription to the person's favorite magazine. If the magazine provides a message line on the address label, mention the employee's achievement there, along with your thanks.

46. It's never too soon to celebrate. On a new employee's first day, give a card that says you are glad she has joined the team and what impressed you about her during the interview process.

47. Sometimes the best recognition is to help resolve a difficult situation. For a person whose child is failing math, perhaps lessons with a personal tutor is the best reward.

48. Improve your employee's working conditions with a new, ergonomically designed chair.

49. When a top performer is going on a particularly long business trip, upgrade her ticket to business class.

50. Stock up on their favorite snacks. Periodically, invite your people to join you for a snack while you talk about how the day is going.

51. Send out one handwritten thank-you note a day to someone who has helped you. You'll be surprised to find that you never run out of people to thank.

52. The best awards align with employee interests. Whenever you visit your people, write down the things you learn about their interests. At award time, you might even thank *us*.

53. Be sure that an award aligns with the achievement. More significant achievements require more significant rewards. In most cases, an underwhelming award is worse than no award at all.

54. Print out and present a team member a "long lunch" certificate for a two-hour break.

55. Like most managers, you have probably witnessed (or experienced firsthand) the tug-of-war between work and home. So why not get on the same side of the rope? The next time an employee goes above and beyond—spending long hours at the office—send a basket of food to his significant other, thanking the family for their sacrifice. (An easy place to do this is at thanks.com.) You do something nice for me, and I appreciate it. But when you do something nice for my family, all of a sudden we are family.

56. Another great way to bridge the gap between family and work is to celebrate the birthdays of employees' children. It doesn't have to be much, but an hour off on the big day will go miles toward creating a positive attitude for the company at home.

57. If you've got a story to tell, your company has a great place to tell it: the company newsletter. Don't worry about spelling or grammar or formatting. Just write it down, and send it to the newsletter people. If they are smart, they'll eat it up. And so will your employee.

58. Give a day pass to an employee's favorite golf course, ski resort, or spa.

59. While you are away on business, arrange recognition for the employees who stay behind. Prepay for lunch to be brought in by a local restaurant, or have the cafeteria deliver coffee and fresh pastries one day. (And don't forget to let an employee use your reserved parking spot while you're away.)

60. Bring something back from your next business trip for each employee as a thank-you. It doesn't have to be expensive, just thoughtful.

61. If you're having trouble getting started with recognition, why not reward yourself after each award presentation? Treat yourself to your favorite snack or drink.

62. Give your employee a personalized ring-tone for her cell phone.

63. To keep motivation at its peak, celebrate service anniversaries as close to the actual day as possible, and

publicly in a small group of peers. You may also want to recognize again at an annual banquet, but the celebration on the date is essential.

64. Rent an employee's dream car for him for a week. Such deals can be negotiated through high-end rental companies. Then take the employee to sign the papers, and let him drive it home.

65. Hire a yard crew to mow an employee's lawn once a week for a month. It will be a long time before the smell of freshly cut grass doesn't make her feel great.

66. Hire a personal chef to prepare dinner for an employee and her family for a night.

67. Hire a maid service for a month for an outstanding employee.

68. Hire a limo to drive your employee to work each day for a week.

Communication (continued)

69. What are you communicating when you're not saying a word? Pay attention to your body language and facial expressions. Are you carrying a big stick, or are you looking for positives?

70. First thing in the morning, spend a moment talking about anything but work with each of your people. This communicates your awareness of each person's life and goals outside the job.

71. Don't forget that the correct ratio to preserve employee morale, motivation, and commitment is five compliments for every one criticism. A friend of ours in the military once noted, "It takes a whole lot of 'Atta-boys' to make up for just one, 'I'm disappointed.'"

72. Watch an award ceremony on TV, and pay attention to the presenters. Did one do a particularly effective job at making the recognition meaningful and memorable for the recipient? Why? Try to incorporate the same qualities into your own award presentations.

73. To get an award presentation right, put everything else—all the interruptions and distractions—on hold for a moment. Interview coworkers. Find out interesting facts about the year the employee joined the company. Read the employee's file.

74. Part of great recognition is the ability to tell about an achievement in a way that makes listeners care. Go to a storytelling festival, and take lessons from the pros.

75. Sixty seconds and three steps. That's all it takes to provide on-the-spot recognition:

    a. Tell the employee exactly what she did that was right.

    b. Tell her what value or goal she achieved.

    c. Say thanks.

76. A catered department picnic is a great time to send the message about a team success. To create a memory, throw in some company T-shirts.

77. Listen to Martin Luther King's "I Have a Dream Speech." Notice the pictures he paints with words. Practice incorporating word pictures into your conversations with employees.

78. Put your thanks on a billboard. If that's too much of a stretch, consider an ad in the local paper or a trade journal.

79. Kindness counts at the office. If you don't believe us, just ask yourself: Would you do better work for someone you liked and who liked you, or would you prefer to work for someone who is aloof and intimidating?

80. To say thanks in an unforgettable way, have flowers sent to the home: 100 of them. There are Web sites that provide this service inexpensively.

81. The very best speech isn't a speech at all. It's an award presentation. Few actions have more impact on everyone in attendance than gathering employees and rewarding someone for living your company values.

82. Try to call your people by their name every time you speak with them.

83. Here's a good rule of thumb for leaders: praise should be public; criticism should be private.

84. Can you be a little more specific? When it comes to giving praise, you better be sure that you are. General, flippant praise, such as, "You do great work," can actually do more harm than good—showing you have no idea what they have been doing. In a recognition moment, be very clear about what you are recognizing and why.

85. Be timely. The effectiveness of an award is inversely related to the amount of time that goes by. The longer you wait, the smaller the impact will be.

86. Organize a lunchtime table tennis, foosball, or bowling tournament to reward hard work. The team that plays together achieves together.

87. Remember there are no "buts" in recognition. Too often we recognize with statements such as: "Susan, thanks for staying late and getting those invoices out. But, you know, if you had followed company procedure, you would have gotten them out on time and wouldn't have had to stay. But, good job." What does the employee remember? The "but."

88. If you have a particularly bold and fun-loving team, change the words to a popular tune, and hire a local musical group to serenade them at their desks.

89. Appearances count. Before a formal award ceremony, take time to ensure the award is beautifully wrapped (out of the shipping package, and complete with the batteries or other setup required). When presenting the award, hand it to the employee. Do not toss it or slide it across the table. Treating the award with dignity adds to its value.

90. Communicate your regard by giving an employee the use of a company cell phone. Or let the person make an international call to a relative anywhere in the world.

91. The most effective bosses work hard not to come off as "bossy." Make it a habit to say "please," and offer specific thank-yous in every communication with employees. You'll find they really are magic words.

92. Take a top employee to lunch with you to celebrate an achievement, and stay for dessert.

Trust

93. When resources get tight, you might think about cutting back on recognition. Don't. Recognition is what motivates and energizes employees to make things happen. Stepping up recognition in tough times sends the strong message that you trust in employees' ability to turn things around.

94. Once every seven days. That's how often day-to-day praise and recognition need to happen to build a committed, trusting workforce. As it turns out, it's also how often we usually fill our cars with gas. So here's an idea: each time you fill your gas tank, make it a point that same day to fuel initiative and creativity among your people with personal, sincere recognition.

95. The next time one of your folks makes a mistake in an effort to move forward in unfamiliar territory, reward it. By rewarding the courage to try something new, you create a trusting environment where innovation can, and will, occur.

96. Right next to recognition on employees' lists of satisfiers is "feeling in on things that are happening." The next time an issue arises within the company, invite the company president or divisional VP to your staff meeting to answer questions. (Get even more mileage out of the visit by publicly highlighting specific employee accomplishments in front of the executive.)

97. When's the last time you asked one of your people for his opinion? If it has been a while, make today the day you solicit input on a current project. Trusting their judgment and then acting on it is one of the greatest compliments you can give a person.

98. Learn to be an active listener. Practice eye contact. Take notes. Ask follow-up questions. The more you demonstrate that you can be trusted with concerns and ideas, the more your people will open up to you.

99. Saying you are part of a team and acting as if you are part of a team are different things. Many supervisors resist doing certain jobs, even when the team is in a bind. Being willing to pitch in and do whatever is needed whenever it is needed goes a long way toward building trust among teammates.

100. Invite an employee to participate in the interview process for a new person by interviewing for technical skills or personality fit, or by verifying background details. Involving an employee demonstrates a high level of regard and trust.

101. Extend yourself on a personal level. The next time one of your people reaches a performance milestone, invite the person and his or her partner to dinner at a high-end restaurant with you and your spouse or significant other. Present a well-thought-out award toward the end of the evening, along with your sincerest thanks.

102. How long can you keep up appearances? Not nearly long enough if you aren't personally committed to your company values and mission. Make sure your walk is consistent with your talk.

103. Think of the one person in the workforce you trust above anyone else. Set up a time to talk to that person about the relationship between trust and recognition. Ask what kind of recognition has worked for her and what she has learned about rewards over the years.

104. What would it take to convince an employee that you are on his side? That you are part of a team? How about doing his least favorite job for the day? (Actually, it's not a bad idea to use at home either.)

105. Take responsibility for your own mistakes, but share the credit for your successes.

106. Send an e-mail to your CEO or division head outlining an employee's above-and-beyond efforts. Then copy your department on the e-mail.

107. For a person who has demonstrated a consistent ability to exceed expectations, give the gift of trust and autonomy. Ensure her continued success by setting goals together and giving her the tools to self-monitor.

Accountability

108. The responsibility for recognition falls squarely on your shoulders as a direct supervisor. Employees value praise from you more highly than kudos from human resources or even the CEO.

109. Temporarily eliminate the middleman (a.k.a. *you*) by giving an employee the job of interfacing with your boss on her next big project. The opportunity to see and be seen by the big dog is a great reward and a great learning opportunity rolled into one.

110. Dependability is a trait that is often overlooked. Chances are that you have someone on your staff who always does solid work, always meets deadlines, is always there . . . and is rarely recognized. Make it a point to change that today.

111. The company newsletter won't write a story on your great person's accomplishment? Then write it down yourself and make copies. Try tucking it under the windshield wipers of every car in the company parking lot.

112. Want to multiply your thanks? Print up some simple coupons for a free cookie from the cafeteria "in honor of [insert your employee's name here]." On the back side of the coupon, tell the story of her accomplishment. Then hand them out to everyone on your team, and go get some cookies.

113. The next time a customer, vendor, or teammate compliments a person in your department, make a note of it. Ask for details, and record them in a file to be shared again during the person's annual review.

114. Whenever you praise an employee, put your notes in the employee's file to review again during the next performance appraisal. (This is another reason to prepare well for awards.)

115. Dare to give perfect scores in an annual review. We've heard of managers rating excellent employees low to keep raises down. What they don't realize is that it keeps achievement down too. Recognize greatness, and you are guaranteed to see more of it. Ignore it, and it will go away.

116. The next time you meet with a client, take along the employee who has played a significant role in maintaining the account. During the meeting, create ownership by publicly recognizing the employee's recent successes.

117. If you feel as if you are dragging your team along, why not try something different? Push them out front! Giving employees credit for their successes doesn't diminish your accomplishment but magnifies it.

118. Make a star performer the star of your next company video. Even better, use this person in your next print ad.

119. At the end of every year, name your conference room after an exceptional employee. Print up a plaque with the employee's name, and mount it on the door for the year. Be sure to take a photo of the employee in front of the door, and have the picture framed.

120. When you promote someone, make it public. Gather the group together to celebrate the achievement. Take the time to explain what behaviors got the employee there, and express appreciation.

121. Ask your company president to write a personal note to an employee who has made a remarkable contribution. Then have it sent to the employee's home. A handwritten note from the president is thoughtful and will be treasured forever.

122. Post letters of praise from clients and colleagues on a bulletin board in a high-profile location.

123. The next time you go out to lunch as a team, formally toast a recent employee achievement. (Take time in advance to prepare your words.)

124. To celebrate a great organizational achievement like hitting a year-end sales goal, take the senior leadership team outside, and spend the day washing every employee's car in the parking lot. It's a great way to communicate that we are in this together (not to mention that it gives employees a chance to say to the CEO, "Hey, you missed a spot").

125. Ask a stellar employee or team to step into a meeting of the board of directors to receive an award and a round of applause. While this only takes a few minutes of time, it is the ultimate in recognition. And it shows your board members something important about the company and what the employees are accomplishing.

Conclusion

Sustaining the Carrot Principle

We can't count the times we have been asked to come into an organization following a year or two of the latest leadership fad. Employees are certainly suspicious of them. They've come to realize that these crazes are just the flavor of the month. Line managers too have become accustomed to being human yo-yos, hearing from on high that a certain leadership initiative is critical today, while suspecting that it will be replaced by something declared just as important tomorrow.

Why do these fads lose momentum? Because they are *ways* to do business, and at best these activity-based programs provide only a short-term boost to productivity. A principle, however, is not a program. It's not an activity. It's a constant.

Unlike a fad or a trend, the Carrot Principle doesn't go out of style every few years. It endures and can be applied in many ways.

Recognition accelerates business results. It amplifies the effect of every action and quickens every process. It also heightens your ability to see employee achievements, sharpens your communication skills, creates cause for celebration, boosts trust between you and your employees, and improves accountability.

Deb Gondek at Rich Products Corp. told us, "It would be impossible for us to know every impact recognition is having on our bottom line because there are so many. But what we do know is that recognition is inspiring associates to realize savings and improvement opportunities that have resulted in millions of dollars of revenue, reduced expenses, increased productivity, and significantly improved gross margins that will continue for years to come."

She adds, "Admittedly, creating a focused recognition strategy takes an incredible amount of time to design and launch a program correctly, but it is worth it. You know you've nailed it when everyone in the organization feels that regardless of their role and level, they can make a difference and feel inspired to do so. You take recognition from an entitlement to an aspiration."

Indeed, recognition at Rich's is becoming a bigger part of corporate culture than anyone expected.

"I am most proud that recognition is starting to become more of a natural thing," says Shari Rife, manager of creative process and facilitation at Rich's. "At first, we constantly had to remind people to think about it. But over the past year, it's become a natural way of thinking. Recognition is becoming a behavior, and that makes all the difference in the levels of engagement and satisfaction we're trying to affect."

Understand that things were good at Rich's before the GEM recognition program was initiated. Turnover was well under the average for the industry, customers were happy, and the company was profitable. Still, to stay competitive, the company set a goal to retain high-performing associates and drive profitable growth. Employee surveys showed that retention and performance would improve if managers recognized more frequently and in more meaningful ways. What created the mandate? Numbers. At Rich's, as at any other organization, numbers matter. Numbers drive initiatives. Numbers validate performance.

One of the goals in *The Carrot Principle* has been to give

you the numbers you need to create a strong case for incorporating or enhancing recognition in your management style and in your organization. Based on research from more than 200,000 interviews, *The Carrot Principle* has illustrated the undeniable correlation between recognition and organizational and individual manager success.

As our research shows, managers rated as "very effective" at recognition by their employees were also rated as:

- Better goal setters

- Better communicators

- More trustworthy

- Able to hold people accountable

Our research leaves no doubt that recognition is the missing ingredient in successful leadership of groups with higher trust, teamwork, productivity, and overall success. In fact, the Ph.D. statisticians at The Jackson Organization have concluded the correlation is so strong that it is statistically *impossible* to be considered a trusted, communicating, team-building, goal-setting manager unless you are effectively using praise and recognition.

This recently became very clear to the new director of technology we interviewed at a start-up company in Silicon Valley. He explained that one evening, just before leaving the office, he received several e-mails from his newly hired system administrator. The language in each message grew increasingly frantic. In short, the system administrator was feeling overwhelmed by the constant change and demands at the evolving company. After just a few weeks, the employee was frustrated and questioning his decision to join the firm, so the new director explained that he went to his system administrator's office to talk. After listening for a while to the concerns, the leader helped the new person narrow his focus to several key job functions. That helped a little. But the thing that made all the difference, he recalled, was his expression of confidence in his employee's abilities.

"I listened for a while, but Glen was still frustrated, I could tell. So I just said, 'Hey, money's short. We aren't going to be able to spend the money on hardware and tools like we'd like. In network terms, we're asking you to take five loaves and two fishes and feed a thousand. We need you to work a technical miracle. I hired you because I know you have the skills to do that.'"

According to the director, that was the moment when the tension broke and the employee started to smile.

"It was amazing," said the leader. "Of course, I've had to follow up with frequent positive validation and recognition. A Carrot Culture needs constant watering."

The director concluded his tale by explaining that Glen's wife had stopped by the office a few weeks later. After shaking the boss's hand, she said, "This job has been great for our family. It's nice to have a husband who is excited to go to work every day and comes home happy."

If you think this story is uncommon, think again. We have seen the Carrot Principle used in every imaginable environment, and on our own team. The Carrot Principle, when applied correctly, works every time. Even in a high-stress environment. Even when funds are low and demands are constant, a manager can build a Carrot Culture using the Carrot Principle. Ensure that your compensation and benefits are fair and equitable, but after that, you must learn to manage with carrots.

And as a manager, the best way to begin a recognition program is just to begin. Keep it focused on a few core goals you want to further. Keep it simple. But most important, don't wait for the organization to create a formal program to follow. Never forget:

The best Carrot Cultures
are owned manager by manager.

Over the past decade, we have had the privilege to work with and learn from some amazing managers. In fact, we have dedicated our careers to the Carrot Principle, detailing it in our books, consulting, speaking, and training. We simply can't abide the idea of workplaces where people feel undervalued, underappreciated, and that their talents are underused—especially when the remedy is so obvious and so much fun.

And yet with all of the empirical evidence of the impact of recognition, why do so many managers hesitate to begin? Perhaps because recognition can feel so awkward at first. It reminds us of two recent documentaries on space travel set to run back to back in theaters. In the first, new astronauts in training tripped, fell, and toppled as they experienced a weightless atmosphere for the first time. It was comical, and most audiences chortled throughout. In the next film, the crowd grew quiet as they watched an astronaut repair a space shuttle from outside the craft, displaying pinpoint accuracy under intense pressure and zero gravity.

The difference between the two experiences? Time and practice.

It's the same with recognition.

In the beginning, recognition can feel awkward, disorienting, unnerving. But our advice is to keep with it. Start by writing a few handwritten, specific thank-you notes at the end of the day today, and see how they are received. Start by calling your employees together once a week and presenting an award to someone who has gone above and beyond. Start by making a great formal presentation of the next service award in your group.

In time, what was once comical becomes perfected. You gain experience and greater skill until you have mastered the Carrot Principle, and as you do, you'll find the celebration of one success launches a thousand more. It works like this. You notice and reward your people's actions that further your goals and their own. Employees are recognized and see their peers receive recognition. People focus more intently on the behaviors that bring rewards, the very behaviors that are most important to your organization. Your organization moves closer to executing its goals. You provide further recognition. Employees further improve their performance and move closer to achieving their goals. And the process begins again.

In this way, the Carrot Principle leads you, your employees, and your company on to continued success and achievement. It enhances your potential. Most important, it gives you, as a manager, the power to invent your own future.

Using the Carrot Principle, it is possible to create a team where *almost* is replaced by *above and beyond,* where *close* be comes *on target.*

And as for being *nearer?* We believe you'll find that after all those years of teetering on the edge, it feels immensely satisfying to finally *accelerate.*

APPENDICES

Appendix A:

Acceleration
to Business Results

As *The Carrot Principle* illustrates, the greatest challenge for leaders in growing their firms is not introducing a revolutionary strategy but engaging employees in *executing* their current strategy, no matter what it is. After working with thousands of organizations worldwide and leading the research into recognition-driven leadership, the O. C. Tanner Company has developed a universal recognition effectiveness model that builds on the Carrot Principle to enhance employee engagement and create real business results.

Recognition Effectiveness Model

Basic Four	Recognition Accelerator	Business Results
Goal Setting	*"Recognizing What Matters Most"* **Alignment** – *does it reinforce…* • Desired Culture • Company Values • Business Objectives	**Manager Relevance** ↓
Communication		**Employee Engagement** ↓
Trust		**Business Results**
Accountability	*"Recognizing People the Right Way"* **Impact** – *is it…* • Inclusive • Meaningful • Performance-Based	• Retention • Productivity • Customer Satisfaction • Profitability

METHODOLOGY

Measure → **Assess** → **Design** → **Train** → **Execute**

The foundational element of this model stems from the research presented in this work—that goal setting, communication, trust, and accountability are the Basic Four elements of effective management.

Next, the model outlines the introduction of the accelerant, recognition, to increase manager relevance and employee engagement. It also introduces the two critical factors of effective recognition: alignment and impact. To boost engagement and create business results, recognition must have:

- Alignment with what matters most in an organization—desired culture, company values, and business objectives

- Impact through recognizing people the right way—having well-understood, inclusive programs; creating human and personal recognition experiences that are meaningful to employees; and ensuring recognition is performance based.

Just as this refinement process is constant and never ending, so are the results. The downward arrows in the chart illustrate the stages of success that a company can experience as it follows the recognition effectiveness model. It begins with a manager providing effective recognition for achievement of strategic behaviors and goals. As a result, the manager becomes more significant, more relevant, to employees' individual success and achievement. This heightened manager relevance creates an environment where a leader can reinforce organizational goals through continued recognition, resulting in employees who are not only bonded to their manager but engaged with the organizational vision and goals. When employees are engaged at this level in the activities that support critical goals, and are mentally and emotionally connected with their leaders and the organization, continued recognition creates measurable business results, such as retentions, productivity, customer satisfaction, and profitability.

Rarely, if ever, is recognition perfected at introduction. Therefore, the model includes a proprietary methodology to guide the continuous process of program evaluation and refinement:

* Measure employee engagement and satisfaction and manager relevance levels.

* Assess current recognition efforts to determine what is working and what can be improved.

* Design structured integrated, practical recognition solutions.

* Train managers to use the tools that will embed recognition in your culture.

- Execute by introducing and managing plan elements including ongoing communication, and formal and informal recognition programs.

Applying O. C. Tanner's recognition effectiveness model to your organization's unique vision and goals can create heightened employee engagement and improved business results.

Appendix B:

The Jackson Organization's National Employee Database

Whenever one encounters statistics of any kind, the first action should be to question the validity of the data. This can be a bit more complex than it looks on the surface, as validity is influenced by a wide range of factors: sample size (number of respondents), freshness of the data (When were these data collected, and over what period of time?), response rate (How many people did, or did not, respond to the survey?), survey design (What questions were asked, and why?), and relevance of the data (What correlations did the study identify?).

So how does The Jackson Organization's database measure up? Solid as a rock.

Who Is in the Database?

The Jackson Organization's national database comprises 166 organizations across the United States and represents 220,061 employees. This number is more than enough to provide solid statistical validity. To put these numbers in perspective, public polling for presidential races typically surveys only one thousand to three thousand people out of more than one hundred million voters, yet they can still predict the outcome of a race with remarkable accuracy. With 221,061 employee respondents, the error range is 0.2 percent at the 95 percent confidence level. In other words, if 100 samples of 100 employees each were randomly chosen from the entire employee population, 95 times out of 100, the total results obtained would vary by no more than ±0.2 percentage points from the results than would be obtained if all employees were grouped together.

What Kinds of Data Does the Database Contain?

The variety of respondents in the database lends great depth to employee research. The following is a breakdown of the 166 organizations in the study:

14%	Fewer than 200 employees
24%	200 to 499 employees
20%	500 to 999 employees
19%	1,000 to 1,999 employees
23%	More than 2,000 employees

"Our national database is very balanced. The even spread of respondents across organizations of many different sizes allows for increased confidence in the analyses," said Allan Acton, senior vice president for The Jackson Organization. "And not just for size of an organization, either. There is a 63/37 percent ratio of urban to rural organizations in the database. The database contains organizations of different sizes, locations, and environments."

Freshness of the data is paramount to validity. The database contains only data gathered within a two-year window, with old data thrown out and new data rolled in each quarter. "The work environments across the nation are constantly changing, and the expectations of employees are part of a constantly evolving scene. Data from more than three years ago might mean something quite different now. Technology changes, management and leadership styles change—keeping the data limited to a two-year window ensures that apples are being compared to apples and oranges to oranges," said Acton.

Response rate is among the strongest indicators of a study's validity. Statisticians agree that a survey must have a response rate of at least 50 percent to be considered scientifically valid. "With a response rate less than 50 percent, you encounter what's known as nonresponse bias. If there are more people in a group not responding, the data cannot be trusted. Those who choose *not* to answer could have radically different perceptions than those who do," stated Acton. The response rate for the data we've used is an astounding 69 percent.

What Questions Were Asked in This National Employee Study and Why?

The national database includes questions whose degree of content validity has been repeatedly demonstrated through reasonable and realistic correlation to the dependent variable of overall job satisfaction. Correlation is a statistical technique that can show whether and how strongly pairs of variables are related. For example, let's consider survey questions that focus on employee recognition, trust in leadership, and the quality of the cafeteria food. While there is a substantial body of research to support that the first two are highly correlated to overall employee satisfaction, the quality of the cafeteria food is rarely a driver of overall employee satisfaction.

An important aspect of correlation is that a high correlation score does not necessarily prove a causal relationship. For example, height and weight are correlated—tall people are, on average, heavier than short people. However, being heavy does not cause tallness (but it would be nice), and being tall doesn't necessarily cause heaviness. Height and weight are simply two variables that tend to rise and fall with each other.

Correlation is the key driver of action plans. Focusing on the attributes that are highly correlated to overall satisfaction gives the greatest return on investment. In many ways, correlation functions as data "triage." When faced with two issues—employee recognition and vending machine selection, for example—correlation will help guide priorities. Keeping good employees is far more important than having a particular brand of candy bar in the break room.

The main result of a correlation is called the correlation coefficient (or *r*) and ranges from -1.0 to +1.0. The closer *r* is to +1 or -1, the stronger the association of the two variables. If *r* is close to 0, it means there is no relationship between the variables. If *r* is positive, it means that as one variable gets larger the other gets larger. If *r* is negative it means that as one gets larger, the other gets smaller (often called an *inverse correlation*).

Top Predictors of Employee Satisfaction	Correlatio
At work, I have the opportunity to do what I do best every day	.57
My performance is evaluated in a manner that makes me feel positive about working	.55
Conflicts are managed in a way that result in positive solutions	.53
My opinions seem to matter to my manager	.52
My manager shares all the information my co-workers and I need in order to feel part of the team	.52
I receive the information I need to do my job	.52
The organization has developed work/life policies that address my needs	.51
I trust my immediate manager	.51
During the past year, communication between leadership and employees has improved	.51
My manager does a good job of recognizing employee contributions	.50
I have recently received praise or recognition for my work	.50

Satisfaction is a state of mind; engagement is a state of action. Measuring satisfaction alone is not enough. Several studies have suggested that a large percentage of employees are actively disengaged even if they are satisfied. To be successful in providing the highest-quality service to its clients, the organization needs to have a satisfied *and* fully engaged workforce. The national database provides the ability to produce satisfaction verses engagement analyses that facilitate an effective and targeted development of action plans.

- High Satisfaction/High Engagement: With this group, celebrate successes and study and spread best practices.

- Low Satisfaction/High Engagement: This area requires the most attention. These are the people who are giving their all but are not happy with their work environment. The organization is most in danger of losing these top performers.

- High Satisfaction/Low Engagement: These are the folks who are happy to get by. They drain organizational resources.

- Low Satisfaction/Low Engagement: Not satisfied and actively disengaged. This group requires an exhaustive review of management and procedures.

Organizations have long understood the value of measuring employee satisfaction. It is an important tool that helps your company identify employee motivators and the drivers that contribute to employee retention and a stable workforce. These drivers often include pay and benefits, having measurable goals, level of trust with management, recognition of achievements, and development and communication of an organizational vision and strategic plan, to name a few. It is important that businesses measure and understand how they are doing in these areas. Measuring satisfaction and taking action based on those findings helps improve retention and satisfaction and can improve processes and procedures. But organizations can take their research a step further and expand beyond measuring only satisfaction.

Businesses should be using their employee measurement tool as an opportunity to develop a more productive workforce. This can be accomplished by also measuring employee engagement. Engaged employees have been shown to be more loyal to the organization and higher performers who provide more innovation, take responsibility to make things happen, have a desire to contribute to the success of the company, and have an emotional bond to the organization, its mission, and vision.

Satisfaction and engagement reinforce and complement each other. A satisfied employee is more likely to be engaged, and an engaged employee is more likely to be satisfied. However, the value is in looking at both. For example, you will want to identify those employees who are satisfied but not engaged. These employees are coming to work and doing their job, but may not be working at the highest capacity, or they are not proactive in finding other ways to contribute to the organization. On the other hand, an employee may be highly engaged but dissatisfied with her pay, management, or level of resources. Identification of this segment of your workforce is critical as they are your most productive employees; however, your organization may be in danger of losing them since they are not satisfied with certain aspects of the job. A retention effort for this portion of the workforce becomes extremely important as you strive to improve the efficiency of your organization.

By focusing on both satisfaction and engagement, organizations will develop highly productive employees who are strong contributors to the organization. Focusing on the development of these employees contributes to higher customer satisfaction, reduces turnover, increases productivity, and improves profits.

Appendix C:

2006 Survey of 1,005 Working Adults

A lthough The Jackson Organization's 221,061-person research study was conducted with some clients in manufacturing, high-tech, service, and financial industries, the most diverse cross-section of job types, educational levels, and backgrounds was found within health care organizations. In no other trade will you find highly paid administrators, vice presidents, and physicians; midlevel directors, managers, and supervisors; salaried and hourly staff working all sorts of day and night, weekday and weekend shifts; highly technical workers; union employees; maintenance, janitorial, and cafeteria workers; and extensive volunteer networks. And on top of all that, they have a high level of government regulation, pressing deadlines, and the stress of knowing that a mistake can cost a customer's life. As a result, much of the original research for *The Carrot Principle* was conducted within health care organizations

To prove these results across a statistically balanced general population, The Jackson Organization followed its major research with a 1,005-person study in 2006 to test these results with working people in all industries, including high-tech, manufacturing, automotive, trades, transportation, construction, media, energy, government, education, services, entertainment, pharmaceuticals, banking, and finance. The link between recognition, engagement, and satisfaction was readily apparent in the consumer study.

The phone survey was conducted in April 2006 with 1,005 working adults throughout the United States. Respondents were asked a series of engagement, satisfaction, and recognition questions that were asked on the core study. This survey proved the larger study data with a scientifically valid cross-section of job types in all industries. It achieved its goal with a margin of error of ±0.5% at a 95 percent confidence rate. In addition to confirming the findings of the major study, it added some unique perspectives on the role of recognition in the employee work experience.

To reach some new conclusions, the researchers developed a recognition index, an average rating for the following three questions in the survey:

- My manager does a good job of recognizing my contributions.

- I have recently received praise or recognition for my work.

- My manager recognizes excellence.

The following charts outline how overall satisfaction, morale, engagement, and employee retention are influenced by the recognition index. The columns on the far right represent the top quartile (top 25 percent) of recognition index scores. All four charts clearly show that as recognition increases (from left to right), overall satisfaction, morale, engagement, and employee retention also increase.

The driving force of recognition is strongest for morale and engagement as the move from the third quartile to the highest quartile for recognition signifies a jump of more than 50 percent for these two key indicators.

Percentage of Employees "Completely Satisfied" with Their Jobs
By Level of Recognition (n=1,005)

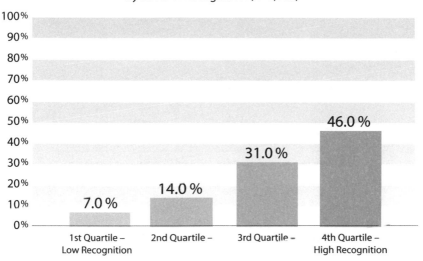

Percentage of Employees Who "Completely Agree" That Their Morale Is Very High
By Level of Recognition (n=1,005)

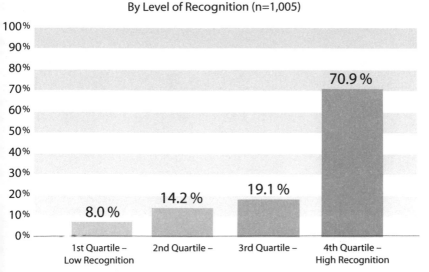

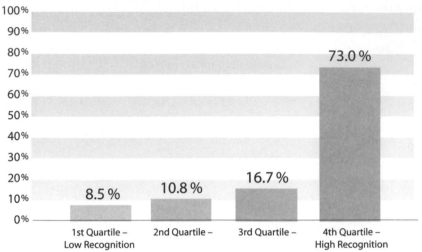

Percentage of Employees Who Are "Highly Engaged"
By Level of Recognition (n=1,005)

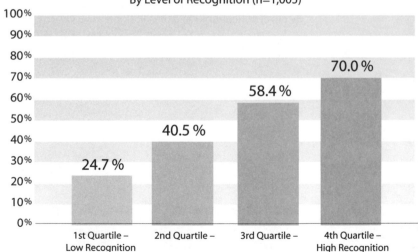

**Percentage of Employees with
"Very High" Desire to be Working for Their Current Employer
One Year from Now**
By Level of Recognition (n=1,005)

In addition to these remarkable data culled from the responses, the survey uncovered some interesting qualitative research that adds more validity to our work. At the end of the survey, respondents were asked the following question: "Other than salaries, staffing, or benefits, if you were your company president, what two things would you do to make your workplace better for employees?" *Recognition/appreciation* was the second most common response after *better teamwork and communication.*

The top four responses are listed below in order of frequency:

1. Better teamwork and more communication

2. More recognition and appreciation

3. Improve the workplace/facility

4. Better, more visible management

The demographic breakdown of the respondents to this survey were well within national statistical ranges:

Education

High school graduate or less	25 percent
Technical, trade school, or some college	31 percent
College/university complete	29 percent
Postgraduate work	15 percent

Age

Under 34	26 percent
35 to 44	24 percent
45 to 54	30 percent
55 and older	20 percent

Occupation

Professional/technical	39 percent
Clerical/service	18 percent
Tradesman/machine operator/laborer	15 percent
Middle manager	11 percent
Sales and marketing	9 percent
Upper management	6 percent
Did not respond	2 percent

Appendix D:

Recognition ROI Survey of 26,000 Employees

Forming a summary of data from 26,000 employees at all career levels, the Recognition ROI study examined thirty-one organizations of varying size and profitability. The Jackson Organization partnered with us to summarize and publish this research on May 25, 2005.

The research focuses on one common question that was addressed in every survey given to the 26,000 people. The respondents were asked to rate, on a scale from low to high, their level of agreement with the following statement: "My organization recognizes excellence." A mean score of all employees from the same organization was then taken. Based on this score, the companies were rated and placed into one of four quartiles:

- Bottom: The bottom 25 percent of companies with employees claiming the lowest level of agreement to the statement, "My organization recognizes excellence."

- Second to the bottom: The second-to-the-bottom 25 percent of companies with employees claiming the second-to-the-lowest-level of agreement to the statement, "My organization recognizes excellence."

- Third to the bottom: The second-to-the-top 25 percent of companies with employees claiming second to the highest level of agreement to the statement, "My organization recognizes excellence."

- Top: The top 25 percent of companies with employees claiming the highest level of agreement to the statement, "My organization recognizes excellence."

Each quartile was then compared against the following three profitability measures:

- Return of equity (a fiscal year's earnings divided by the average shareholder's equity for that year): This measurement is used as a general indication of how much profit a company is able to generate from the investment provided by its shareholders.

- Return on assets (a fiscal year's earnings divided by total assets): This number tells how much a company has achieved for each dollar of assets utilized.

- Operation margin (the ratio of operating income to sales): This shows how much a company makes from each dollar of sales before interest and taxes.

The startling results showed companies in the top quartile (companies with the highest mean scores from their employees' agreement to the statement, "My organization recognizes excellence") earned a significantly higher return on equity, return on assets, and operating margin. For detailed results, please refer to chapter 1 of this book.

The thirty-one organizations in this study were health care organizations, a solid proving ground for this research since in no other industry is there such variety (for example, of pay levels, job types, union and nonunion employees, technical workers, shift variances). The researchers have worked with organizations in high-tech, financial services, manufacturing, and other industries and estimate with good faith that these results would not be statistically different in other industries, as was evidenced with the correlation of recognition to employee engagement and satisfaction in the general consumer study outlined in Appendix C.

NOTES

1: A Missing Ingredient

Page

3   "Striding home from the local mercantile . . ." Background on Charles Goodyear was found in the following:

- Steven Caney. *Invention Book*. New York: Workman Publishing, 1985.

- National Geographic Society. *Inventors and Discoverers: Changing Our World*. Washington, D.C.: National Geographic Society, 1988.

- James Dyson. *A History of Great Inventions*. New York: Carroll & Graf Publishers, 2001.

- Harold Evans. *They Made America*. New York: Little, Brown, 2004.

- "The Charles Goodyear Story," which can be found in the "Corporate History" section of Goodyear.com. www.goodyear.com/corporate/history

8   "The fact is that 79 percent of employees who quit their jobs . . ." Society for Human Resource Management *1997 Retention Practices Survey*. Alexandria, Va.: Society for Human Resource Management, 1997.

8   "Sixty-five percent of North Americans report . . ." Tom Rath. "65% of Americans Receive No Praise or Recognition in the Workplace." News release issued via e-mail from the Gallup Organization's bucketbook.com, August 18, 2004.

9   "In fact one-third of the people you give a cash award . . ." "Navigating the Incentive Construction Zone: Motivating with Merchandise and Travel Makes More Sense Than Ever." *Potentials,* May 2000, quoting Wirthlin Worldwide study conducted for American Express Incentive Services.

10   "When people join us . . ." Quoted in David Mason Jones. "What Employees Really Want," *HRM Singapore,* May 12, 2005.

12   "According to author Fred Reichheld . . ." Fred Reichheld and Thomas Teal. *Loyalty Effect.* Boston: Harvard Business School Press, 2001.

12   "Turnover is an estimated $5 trillion annual drain . . ." This and other sources in this paragraph are found in: Frederic Frank, Richard Finnegan, and Craig Taylor. "The Race for Talent: Retaining and Engaging Workers in the 21st Century." *Human Resources Planning,* September 1, 2004.

13   "The Society for Human Resource Management periodically . . ." Citing Society for Human Resource Management. 2000 *Retention Practices Survey.* Alexandra, Va.: Society for Human Resource Management, 2000.

13   "A fascinating survey has been conducted three times . . ." James Kouzes and Barry Posner. *Encouraging the Heart.* San Francisco: Jossey-Bass, 1999.

14   "A Watson Wyatt Reward Plan Survey of 614 employers . . ." Watson Wyatt, "Linking Pay Strategy to Business Goals Boosts the Bottom Line." Press release, November 18, 1997, which can be found in the News section at watsonwyatt.com.

14   " . . . Gallup's study of nearly 5 million employees . . ." From Tom Rath and Donald Clifton. *How Full Is Your Bucket.* Gallup Press, New York City, August 2004.

15   "Research firm Watson Wyatt has asked . . ." Protective Ser-

vices Training Institute of Texas. "Enhance Motivation." In *Protection Connection,* version 102, which can be found in the Research section at utexas.edu.

2: The Basic Four of Leadership

Page

30   "... in a recent survey by Right Management Consultants ..." "Survey: Unknown Strategies Lead to Employee Disengagement." *Chief Learning Officer,* February 8, 2006.

31   "Some 67 percent of the organizations surveyed either ..." World at Work staff, "Biggest Reason for Disengaged Employees: Failure to Explain Why They Are There," February 9, 2006, e-mailed press release from World at Work organization, Scottsdale, Arizona, quoting research from Right Management Consultants.

31   "Jack Welch, retired CEO of General Electric ..." Noel Tichy and Stratford Sherman. *Control Your Destiny or Someone Else Will: How Jack Welch Is Making General Electric the World's Most Competitive Corporation.* New York: Doubleday, 1993.

32   "As Bill George, former chairman and CEO of Medtronic ..." Bill George. *Authentic Leadership.* San Francisco: Jossey-Bass, 2003

34   "Paul Zak, professor of economics at Claremont University ..." Jerry Adler. "Mind Reading: The New Science of Decision Making. It's Not as Rational as You Think." *Newsweek,* July 5, 2004.

34   "That's what Watson Wyatt Worldwide found when they surveyed 7,500 ..." Watson Wyatt Worldwide, Washington, D.C. *WorkUSA 2000 Survey.*

34   "Louis Barnes, professor emeritus at Harvard ..." Louis Barnes. "Managing the Paradox of Organizational Trust." *Harvard Business Review,* March 1, 1981.

3: Leadership Accelerated

Page

39   "Research by Edward L. Deci and his colleagues . . ." Edward Deci and Richard Ryan. *Intrinsic Motivation and Self-Determination in Human Behavior.* New York: Plenum, 1985.

39   "Leadership gurus Kouzes and Posner describe . . ." James Kouzes and Barry Posner. *Encouraging the Heart.* San Francisco: Jossey-Bass, 1999.

40   " 'The childhood need to "be there now" . . . ' " Kenneth Thomas. *Intrinsic Motivation at Work: Building Commitment and Energy.* San Francisco: Berrett-Koehler.

46   " 'This innate need for appreciation is not a selfish . . . ' " Terrence Deal and M. K. Key. *Corporate Celebration: Play, Purpose, and Profit at Work.* San Francisco: Berrett-Koehler, 1998.

4: Altruists and Expectors

Page

58   "Abraham Maslow's *Hierarchy of Needs* . . ." Abraham Maslow. *Motivation and Personality,* 2nd. ed. New York: Harper & Row, 1970.

60   " . . . work was once seen as human penance . . ." Gayle Porter. "Work, Work Ethic, Work Excess." *Journal of Organizational Change Management,* September 1, 2004.

61   "In fact, some 25 million U.S. workers today report . . ." Joanne Gavin and Richard Mason. "The Virtuous Organization: The Value of Happiness in the Workplace." *Organizational Dynamics,* December 2004.

64   "As Brook Manville and Josiah Ober explained . . ." Brook Manville and Josiah Ober. "Beyond Empowerment." *Harvard Business Review,* January 2003 (emphasis added).

65   "Not only do increased work hours over a certain point . . ." "Challenging Time Poverty," which can be found at simpleliving. net/timeday.

66 " . . . acknowledgment and support of life goals . . ." Thomas Wright and Russell Cropanzano. "The Role of Psychological Well-Being in Job Performance." *Organizational Dynamics,* December 2004.

5: Creating a Carrot Culture

Page

76 " . . . a Wichita State University poll . . ." Gerald H. Graham, *Understanding Human Relations: The Individual, Organization, and Management.* New York: SRA/McGraw-Hill Publishing Company, May 1982.

83 " . . . 2006 survey of 14,000 workers, showing 65 percent . . ." Reuters wire story, January 30, 2006.

6: Are They Engaged *and* Satisfied?

Page

85 " . . . customers who have a negative experience tell . . ." Dale Zetocha. "Retaining Customers by Handling Complaints." Michigan State University Extension Tourism Education materials, which can be found at the Michigan State University Extension Web site at msue.msu.edu.

7: The Building Blocks of a Carrot Culture

Page

98 " . . . the reason most mergers fail is culture clash . . ." *Bank Director First Quarter,* January 1, 2002, YellowBrix, Inc.

98 " . . . more than two out of three mergers fail . . ." Karen Lowry Miller. "With the World Caught up in Merger Mania Again, Studies Suggest Few Tie-ups Will Fail, This Time." *Newsweek International,* April 24, 2006.

99 " 'We often ask audiences if they think their companies . . . ' " Jack Welch and Suzy Welch. "Keeping Your People Pumped." *Business Week,* March 27, 2006.

100   "Authors Deal and Key explain the . . ." Terrence Deal and M.K. Key. *Corporate Celebration: Play, Purpose, and Profit at Work.* San Francisco: Berrett-Koehler, 1998.

110   "Towers Perrin has found that 86 percent . . ." Towers Perrin, "Largest Single Study of the Workforce Worldwide Shows That Employee Engagement Levels Pose a Threat to Corporate Performance Globally," news bulletin, November 15, 2005, which can be found at towersperrin.com.

117   " . . . are used by more than 90 percent . . ." Citing "Trends in Employee Recognition 2005," a survey of members of World at Work and the National Association for Employee Recognition, May 2005, which can be found at www.recognition.org.

118   " . . . three out of four U.S. workers are not loyal . . ." Steve Bates. "Workers' Loyalty to Employers Rising, Survey Finds." November 21, 2005. This can be found on HR News at SHRM.org.

118   "Quint Studer in his book, *Hardwiring Excellence* . . . " Quint Studer. *Hardwiring Excellence.* New York: Fire Starter Publishing, 2003.

120   "Remember the words of Henry David Thoreau . . ." Henry David Thoreau. "Life Without Principle." *Atlantic Monthly,* October 1863.

8: Carrotphobia: Why We Don't Recognize

Page

126   "Another angle on this is from leadership experts . . ." Jack Welch and Suzy Welch. "Keeping Your People Pumped." *Business Week,* March 27, 2006.

130   " . . . business is fast discovering that monetary rewards . . ." D. Fonville. "Hungry for Productivity?" *Richmond Times-Dispatch,* April 1, 2000.

O. C. Tanner Recognition Company

For more than eighty years, the O. C. Tanner Company has been the world's leading provider of employee recognition solutions. Serving thousands of the world's most successful companies, O. C. Tanner offers recognition awards; strategic solutions for employee motivation; the latest in recognition best practices; and high-tech, online recognition tools. To learn more, visit www.octanner.com.

The Jackson Organization

Much of the vital quantitative research for this book was compiled by The Jackson Organization of Laurel, Maryland. The Jackson Organization was founded in 1997 by Dave Jackson, a former senior vice president of the Gallup Organization. Over the past decade, Jackson has been among the fastest-growing research companies in the nation.

The Jackson Organization is a full-service market research firm that offers a unique combination of customized research and market expertise. Working with each client, this leading research firm delivers research solutions that will result in positive business outcomes: higher profitability, improved productivity, greater market share, and lower turnover. To learn more, visit www.jacksonorganization.com.

ACKNOWLEDGMENTS

In writing *The Carrot Principle,* we stood on the shoulders of many talented people—so many, in fact, that it's hard to know where to begin to express our gratitude, except, perhaps, at the place where this book began: with the research.

During a speaking engagement at Orange Regional Medical Center, we stumbled on The Jackson Organization, independent market researchers. Allan Acton of Jackson was presenting the results of a recently concluded employee attitude survey at the hospital. We were there to speak on recognition, which the center hoped to improve. Over the next year as we worked together to enhance Orange Regional's culture, we also began the in-depth analysis this work would require. Throughout the writing of this book, The Jackson Organization has allowed us unprecedented access to its rich database. Much gratitude is due to David Jackson, Allan Acton, Berke Bilbay, Craig Calvert, Rebecca Schwoch, and Karen Endresen.

Soon after meeting The Jackson Organization, serendipity struck again. One Sunday, we were profiled in the *New York Times* business section. The article concluded that while our books might be popular around the world, in the United States we were not yet household names. Fred Hills, from Simon & Schuster, called us that weekend. When we pitched the vision of this work, everyone at Simon & Schuster was quick to embrace the concept. For their guidance, we thank our tenacious editor, Emily Loose, as well as Fred Hills, Martha Levin, Suzanne Donahue, Michele Jacob, Carisa Hays, Tom Spain, and the rest of the team. They have helped us create a work in which we take great pride.

Meanwhile, our decade-long relationship with the O. C. Tanner Company continued to provide an endless stream of knowledge, insight, and case studies, allowing us to put faces on the Jackson Organization research numbers. We are indebted to the recognition consultants and thought leaders at O. C. Tanner, including Kent Murdock, David Petersen, Carolyn Tanner Irish, David Sturt, Tim Treu, John McVeigh, Brian Katz, Kevin Salmon, Gary Beckstrand, Bill Grubbs, Michelle Barneck, Alex Goble, Clark Campbell, Kaye Jorgensen, Kevin Curtis, Greg Boswell, Bill Adams, David Hilton, Rob Mukai, Ty Brown, Joyce Anderson, Gail Bedke and her team, Pam Basone, Amy Skylling, Shauna Raso, BJ Beckman, Mary Steadman, Jason Andersen, Ashley Broadhead, Sarah Orellana, Cordell Clinger, and Scott Brown. We relied on the following O. C. Tanner regional consultants who had established strong relationships with their clients: Kim Purcell, Jim Vincenzi, Tom Meyer, Dan Norman, Tom Rosato, Jim Mulhern, Mike Bruce, John Robinson, Tom Long, Bruce Darrington, Dan Challis, John Cassell, Debbie Phipps, Larry Farris, and Steve Johnson. We also thank the regional vice presidents, executives, employees, and the board of directors.

As always, the Carrot Culture Group—featuring the amazing Angie Haugen, Scott Christopher, Max Brown, Bob Ann Hall, Chad Johnson, and Wylie Thomas—pulled together to support and vastly enhance our efforts. An adjunct member of that group is our brilliant graphic consultant, Richard Sheinaus, of Gotham Design in New York City.

With the book nearing completion, colleagues from around the country were recruited as critical readers. Among them were Glen Nelson, Christie Giles, and Mindi Cox, as well as many of those we have mentioned in the Carrot Culture Group, those at The Jackson Organization, and at the O. C. Tanner Company. This work is stronger because of their probing questions and attention to detail.

The writing of this book has taken us into the hearts and minds (and balance sheets) of many organizations. We are grateful to our contacts at the firms we have included: Sylvia Brandes, Joe Maiorano, and Margaret Teegan at KPMG; Rosemary Boggs, Jody Brown, and Jack London at CACI; Quint Studer of the Studer Group; David Kasiarz, Steve Stalder, Jennifer Elliott, Amy Polacko, Henry Patton, and Roger Carey at the Pepsi Bottling Group; Xcel Energy's Bill Newby and John Torres; Scott Northcutt, Joan Kelly, Perry Belcastro, and Rosemarie Magrone at DHL; Ed Zobeck and Ann Federici at the Auto Club Group; Cheryl Hutchinson and Beverly Gomez at Friendly Ice Cream Corporation; Rich Products Corp.'s Deb Gondek, Shari Rife, Maria Grimaldi, Tom Hauser, Janice Horn, and Maureen Hurley; Chuck Dwyer and Douglas Bottrill at HSBC Bank Canada; and Lynette Butler, Bruce Jensen, and Bill Nelson at Intermountain Health Care.

It is difficult to believe (given our youthful good looks) that we have spent the greater part of the past fifteen years spreading the word about *The Carrot Principle* around the world. Still today, our confidence in the transforming power of this principle continues to grow. We appreciate all the people who have invited us into their companies to speak and train on recognition-driven leadership and those who have trusted us to speak to their conference audiences.

We also owe a great deal of gratitude to all those managers who practice these concepts, making a real difference in the lives of those they lead.

Finally, we must again thank our families, to whom we dedicate this work. To Jennifer and Tony. To Heidi, Cassi, Carter, Brinden, and Garrett.

INDEX

ABOUT THE AUTHORS

We'd love to hear your success stories with the Carrot Principle. Please visit carrots.com for further details. While you are there, you can learn more about recognition-driven leadership.

Adrian Gostick is the author of several successful books including the *New York Times* best seller *The Invisible Employee*. He also wrote the *Wall Street Journal* and *Business Week* best seller *A Carrot a Day*; *The Integrity Advantage*; and *The 24-Carrot Manager*, which has been called a "must read for modern-day managers" by Larry King of CNN. Adrian's books have been translated into fifteen languages and are sold in more than fifty countries around the world. As an employee motivation expert, he has appeared on network television programs and has been quoted in dozens of business publications and magazines. He is managing director of the Carrot Culture Group, a consulting and training division of O. C. Tanner Company, where he works with organizations to build effective employee recognition programs. Adrian earned a master's degree in strategic communication and leadership from Seton Hall University, where he is a guest lecturer on organizational culture. You can reach him at adrian@carrots.com.

Chester Elton coauthored *The Invisible Employee*, a *New York Times* best seller; *Managing with Carrots*, which was nominated as the Society of Human Resource Management (SHRM) Book of the Year; *The 24-Carrot Manager;* and *A Carrot a Day.* As a motivation expert, Chester has been featured in the *Wall Street Journal, Washington Post,* and *Fast Company* magazine; has been profiled in the *New York Times;* and was called "an apostle of appreciation" by the *Globe and Mail* (Canada). He has been a guest on NBC's *Today Show,* CNN's *Business Unusual,* and on National Public Radio. A sought-after speaker and recognition consultant, Chester is vice president of performance recognition with the O. C. Tanner Recognition Company. He has spoken to audiences throughout the world and was the highest-rated speaker at the 2005 SHRM annual conference. He serves as a recognition consultant to Fortune 500 firms such as Johnson & Johnson, AOL/Time Warner, DHL, Avis, and KPMG. You can reach him at chester@carrots.com.